G. A. Macfarren

Six lectures on harmony

Delivered at the Royal institute of Great Britain, before Easter, 1867

G. A. Macfarren

Six lectures on harmony
Delivered at the Royal institute of Great Britain, before Easter, 1867

ISBN/EAN: 9783741194313

Manufactured in Europe, USA, Canada, Australia, Japa

Cover: Foto ©ninafisch / pixelio.de

Manufactured and distributed by brebook publishing software (www.brebook.com)

G. A. Macfarren

Six lectures on harmony

Ballantyne Press
BALLANTYNE, HANSON AND CO., EDINBURGH
CHANDOS STREET, LONDON

SIX LECTURES

ON

HARMONY.

DELIVERED AT

THE ROYAL INSTITUTION OF GREAT BRITAIN,

Before Easter, 1867.

BY

G. A. MACFARREN.

THIRD EDITION.

LONDON:
LONGMANS, GREEN, & CO.
1882.

TO

MY EARLY FRIEND

G. A. OSBORNE,

THIS BOOK

Is Dedicated

IN

ACKNOWLEDGMENT OF MANY BONDS OF PERSONAL ATTACHMENT,

NOT THE LEAST OF WHICH IS

THAT THE DELIVERY OF THESE LECTURES WAS MAINLY

DUE TO HIM.

G. A. M.

PREFACE

TO

THE FIRST EDITION.

HE that hears music without the ability to discriminate its constituents, resembles one who witnesses a dramatic performance in an unknown foreign language, who may be charmed by the gestures and the elocution of the actors, and even interested in the course of the action, but, understanding not the words that are spoken, must be dead to the poetry of the work. The purpose of these Lectures is to stimulate such persons, if may be, to investigate the elements of a work of musical art, as a means of quickening their perception of its beauties.

The Course is a statement of the lecturer's convictions, which are authorized by the practice of the greatest masters, and are confirmed by his practical experience. They point to the very broad, but not universally recognised, distinctions between the ancient, contrapuntal, artificial style of harmony, comprised in what may be called archaic art in music; and the modern, fundamental, natural style of harmony, comprised in the living art of our own times.

The application of the terms strict and free to these two styles of harmony, throughout the Lectures must not be confounded with other frequent technical uses of the same words. A strict canon, for instance, is one in which the notes of the original part or parts are repeated, either on the same or on other degrees of the scale, note for note, interval for interval, semitone by semitone; whereas, a free canon is one in which minor intervals are occasionally substituted in the answer, for major intervals in the original part, and in like manner tones for semitones. Again, a strict Fugue is one wherein all the stringent laws for its construction are scrupulously fulfilled; whereas, a free Fugue, to which class belong the very great majority of pieces in the fugue form that are now before the public, may supply the general requirements as to the development of a subject, but present very wide exceptions from the accepted prescriptions for fugal composition. On the other hand, the strict and the free styles of harmony are alike available for either a free or strict Canon or Fugue.

The different degrees of musicianship in the audience, and, still more, the inexorable clock of the Royal Institution, compelled a very incomplete treatment of the subject. Readers who may wish to examine more deeply the principles enunciated in these Lectures than was compatible with the occasion of their delivery, are referred to "A Treatise on Harmony," by Alfred Day. Any who may be willing to study practically the theory of music from the point of view herein set forth, may find exercises in the author's "Rudiments of Harmony."

May, 1867.

PREFACE

TO

THE SECOND EDITION.

SINCE the delivery of these Lectures, and the issue of their first edition, the author has learned the fallacy of the tradition therein stated as to the origin of the artificial scales or modes of the Roman Church, which it is the aim of some zealous and well-meaning persons to introduce into the standard use of the Church of England. Not to give even the trifling support of these pages to the perpetuation of that error, the passages are now omitted which identified the Greek with the Ecclesiastical musical system, and which ascribed to St. Ambrose and St. Gregory successive participation in the adoption in the Western Church of the musical scales that were devised subsequent to the later of those two prelates. The passages are here replaced by an account of the discrepancy between the two systems and of the date when the Roman Church scales first obtained acceptance. The author owes his present conviction to Mr. William Chappell's "History of Music," and to conversations with him on the purport of the yet unpublished volume of that work, with ample references to the high authorities for all its novel statements.

In other respects the present is a reprint of the first edition, the views in which have wider exemplification than this volume could contain, in "Eighty Musical Sentences to Illustrate Chromatic Chords," by the author, published since that edition appeared.

November, 1876.

PREFACE

TO

THE THIRD EDITION.

THE present differs only from the second edition in some small, but not slight, typographical corrections and in the addition of a few historical and technical particulars. For very far more ample treatment of the subject of the Second Lecture, the reader is referred to "Counterpoint: a Course of Practical Study," by the author, which has appeared since the issue of the second edition of this book.

January, 1882.

CONTENTS.

LECTURE I.

INTRODUCTORY.

Day's theory. Distinction between harmony and melody. Harmony unknown to the Greeks. Diatonic genus. Chromatic genus. Enharmonic genus. Greek modes—Authentic and Plagal. Ecclesiastical modes—Difference of Ecclesiastical from Greek modes—Dorian, Phrygian, Lydian, Hyper- or Mixo-Lydian. Roman Church modes inapt to the Church of England. B flat. Harmony originated by the Northern Laity. Key—Major, Minor. Names of the seven notes of a key. Close, cadence or fall. Full close. Half close. Interrupted close. Distinction between concord and discord . . . . pp. 1—35

LECTURE II.

THE ANCIENT STRICT OR DIATONIC STYLE.

Distinction between the ancient and modern styles. Diatonic concords. Common chords. Tritone. Triad of the leading-note. Triad of the mediant. Common chords in major keys. Triads of supertonic and mediant in minor keys. Common chords in minor keys. Dominant and submediant in minor keys. Tonic major chord in minor keys. Inversion of concords. Inversion of the diminished triad. Inversion of concords in minor keys. Inversion on minor 7th. Pedals. Sequences. Diatonic discord. Passing notes. Arbitrary alterations of minor scale. Double passing notes. Leap of 3rd. Suspension. Suspended 9th. Suspended 4th. Suspended 5th. Double suspension. Florid figures of melody. Suspension of complete chords. Essential discords. Essential 5th of mediant. Essential 7th. Essential 5th of supertonic. Essential 9th. Relative keys . . . . pp. 36—82

LECTURE III.

THE MODERN FREE OR CHROMATIC STYLE.

Exceptional treatment of tonic, dominant and subdominant. Consecutive 5ths and 8ths. Leading-note. Second inversion of concords—Tonic, Subdominant, Dominant. Distinction between suspended 4th and inverted 5th. Harmonics. Fundamental chords. Exceptional treatment of dominant, supertonic and tonic. Chord of the dominant 7th. Chromatic scale. Chromatic concords—Minor 2nd, Supertonic, Minor chord of Subdominant, Inversion (on subdominant) of diminished triad, Minor 6th. Free passing notes—Appoggiatura pp. 83—121

LECTURE IV.

THE MODERN STYLE—*continued*.

Chromatic chord of the supertonic 7th. Chromatic chord of the tonic 7th. Parallel between supertonic and tonic Chromatic discords. Chord of the dominant minor 9th—resolved on a note of the same chord—resolved on a note of another chord. Chord of the supertonic minor 9th. Chord of the tonic minor 9th. False notation. Enharmonic changes. Modulation into twenty-four keys by enharmonic alterations of the inversions of a chord of the minor 9th . . . . pp. 122—154

LECTURE V.

THE MODERN STYLE—*continued*.

Chord of the dominant major 9th—resolved on a note of the same chord—resolved on a note of another chord. Chord of the supertonic major 9th. Chord of the tonic major 9th. Chord of the dominant 11th—resolved on a note of the same chord—resolved on a note of another chord. Modulation by the chord of the 11th. Chord of the dominant minor 13th—resolved on a note of the same chord—resolved on a note of another chord.

False notation of minor 13th. Distinction between augmented 5th and minor 13th. Enharmonic changes of minor 13th. Chord of supertonic minor 13th. Chord of the tonic minor 13th. Modulation into eighteen keys by enharmonic changes of a chord of the minor 13th . . . . pp. 155—190

LECTURE VI.

THE MODERN STYLE—*concluded*.

Chord of the dominant major 13th—resolved on a note of the same chord. Chord of the supertonic major 13th. Chord of the tonic major 13th—resolved on a note of another chord. Chords of the augmented 6th on minor 6th. Inversion of the augmented 6th. Augmented 6th on minor 2nd. Pedals in the free style. Sub-mediant a root of fundamental chords. Inverted pedals. Extended relationship of keys. Unity of Day's theory. Discrepancies in notation. Conclusion.

pp. 191—225

LECTURES ON HARMONY.

LECTURE I.

INTRODUCTORY.

I AM gratified by the opportunity permitted to me of offering a series of technical Lectures on Music to the members of this Institution, in which matters of science and art are expounded, with the purpose of unfolding their principles and describing the laws through which these operate. It is a frequent practice to give musical lectures, on the contrary, in the form of concerts interspersed with anecdotes of the masters whose compositions they include, with perhaps a chronological notice of the rise and decline of the various styles these compositions exemplify. In pursuing a different course from this, of presenting musical performances with—shall I say—historical illustrations, I trust it may not be vain for me to emulate the pattern of the great men in all departments of knowledge who appear before you at this table; and I shall be proud if I can communicate any insight into musical principles analogous to that which you receive here upon other subjects.

I pre-suppose that the announcement of the theme of these lectures has in some sort prepared you to look rather for instruction than amusement in the series; and, as I shall not pretend to furnish you with amusement, I must appeal to the interest in the technicalities of harmony—which I presume has drawn you hither—for such sympathy with the subject I am about to discuss as may enable me to render acceptable the instructive form in which it will be cast.

I presume further that each member of my audience is forearmed, not only with an interest in the subject I am about to treat, but also with a considerable knowledge of its terminology; at least, I trust that you all are familiar with the names of musical notes, and with any words that are in constant use with persons who have some practical proficiency in any branch of the musical art. I will not weary you, therefore, with explanations of technicalities with which every musical tyro is conversant; but I must tax your patience—I hope not too heavily—in defining some terms that are in less general use, yet must frequently occur in my remarks.

Let me say also in advance, to mature musicians, if any such honour me with their attention, who come less to learn than to 'criticize, that any unfamiliar theoretical views which I may bring forward are not of my own discovery. My late friend, Alfred Day, communicated to me his very original and very perspicuous theory of Harmony, by means of which many obscurities in the subject were cleared that my previous anxious study had vainly sought to penetrate, many discrepancies of principle and practice were reconciled between the writings of profound

<small>Day's theory.</small>

teachers and the works of great masters that had previously perplexed and discouraged me. I am indeed so thoroughly convinced of the truth of Day's theory, and I have derived such infinite advantage from its knowledge in my own practical musicianship, that I should be dishonest to myself and to my hearers were I to pretend to teach any other; and if I could have the good fortune to bring any doubters to share in my conviction, I feel that the satisfaction, the self-reliance, the genuine faith they would thus acquire would be a worthy memorial of the keenly penetrating genius of my friend.

The term harmony belongs not exclusively to music. Its Greek original defines the fitness, propriety, accordance of things; so that we use the word in a primitive rather than a figurative sense, when we speak of harmony among the members of a society —of a harmonious whole, comprising the diverse elements in a work of art. It is employed as a technical term by painters; with whose province, however, I will not interfere by speaking of the signification in which it is understood by them. In music, the word harmony expressly defines a *combination* of notes, in contradistinction to melody, which means a *succession* of notes: the first signifying music which requires several performers—except when such instruments as the pianoforte are employed, whereon many notes may be sounded together; the second, which can be executed by a single voice or any instrument that can yield but one sound at a time: the first expressing music which is written vertically; the

Harmony and melody

key of G, and the ♯F that induces this modulation is marked by an accidental :—

SONATA, Op. 53.—*Beethoven.*

another phrase continues throughout in the key of C, and yet contains an accidental ♯F twice :—

OVERTURE TO DER FREYSCHÜTZ.—*Weber.*

The first of these phrases is Diatonic, because the ♯F belongs to the key of G; the second is Chromatic, because the ♯F does not alter the original key.

The genus I have yet to describe is called Enharmonic. This, with the Greeks, comprised a smaller interval than the semitone—a note, namely, between B and C, higher in pitch than the first, but not so high as the second. The word Enharmonic may perhaps be rendered *inter-harmonic*, and probably implied an intervening *sound*—having the same reference to the ♯B between B and C that in architecture, it has to the *style* between the Corinthian and the Composite.

Enharmonic genus.

I shall have future occasion to discuss the etymology of the names of the other two genera, but may dismiss this term Enharmonic with what has now been said. There are two accounts of the origin of the Enharmonic genus. One refers it to the Eastern and Southern nations who habitually intonate smaller musical intervals than semitones—the Persians, for instance, divide their scale of an octave into eighteen sounds, whereas our modern scale is divisible into no more than twelve (the thirteenth, C, being a repetition of the first):—

The other account ascribes the origin of this genus to a practice of sliding the voice from one to the other note in an interval of a semitone, instead of attacking distinctly the two individual sounds—a practice analogous to the *portamento* of modern singing; and in this sense, though it is never written, the effect of the Enharmonic diesis is employed by no means rarely in the musical performances we daily witness. So far as regards musical notation, it may be said that the word enharmonic denotes the distinction between the several names that may be given to the same sound on a keyed instrument, as ♯C and ♭D; the true distinction between these two notes, which may be articulated by a voice, or on an instrument such as the violin, whose notes are stopped by the fingers, presents a field for wide discussion which must be reserved till a subsequent lecture.

Greek modes.

In the diatonic genus, the Greeks had several modes—or, as we should now call them, scales—differing, as do the scales of our several keys, in being higher or lower than each other, but corresponding, as do our scales, in all having the same distribution of tones and semitones. From the Greek modes, the Dorian may be cited as the standard of all, and it may thus be represented in modern notation :—

The Phrygian mode began from E, and had the same distribution of tones and semitones as the Dorian, which was induced by the addition of a sharp to F and the withdrawal of the flat from B. The Lydian began from ♯F, and had ♯G and ♯C. The Mixo-Lydian began from G, and had ♭B and ♭E. Each of these modes had a collateral mode at the interval of a 4th below, and this was distinguished by the addition of the prefix Hypo (*under*) to the name of the original; so, the Hypo-Dorian may be counted from A with all natural notes, the Hypo-Phrygian from B, with ♯C and ♯F, the Hypo-Lydian from ♯C, with ♯D, ♯F, and ♯G, and the Hypo-Mixo-Lydian from D with ♭B.

The original four modes were styled *Authentic*, and were characterized by the two predominant notes of melodies which were cast in them (equivalent to our Tonic and Dominant) being at the interval of a 5th.

Authentic and plagal.

The four *Hypo* modes were called *Plagal* (or sidewise, or relative), and were characterized by the two predominant notes of melodies which were cast in them being at the interval of a 4th.

These terms Authentic and Plagal have endured to our time, and still denote the same melodic affinity, defining the variable forms of any one melody for the subject and answer of a fugue. The interval of the 5th and its inversion the 4th are distinguished, in modern terminology, by the epithet *perfect*, and it is to be remarked that their distinction was already observed in remotest times, and when many niceties, which are obvious to modern perception, were still unregarded.

Of acceptance less common than the above, were the Æolian mode, whose intervals were counted from F, and the Iastian or Ionian, whose intervals were counted from ♭E, and these, like all the others, had their tones and semitones in the same order as the Dorian. Earlier, in the days of Pindar, the Æolian mode was counted from A, but differed from the Hypo-Dorian in not being plagal.

Ecclesiastical Modes.

A manifest fiction has obtained credence in later times, and in recent years has been brought into prominence, to the effect that St. Ambrose, at the end of the fourth century, and St. Gregory, at the end of the sixth, respectively appropriated the Greek modes to ecclesiastical use and reformed abuses which had corrupted this appropriation. Particular uses, in other matters as well as music, distinguished the Churches of Milan and Rome, of which the two worthies were severally bishops, and men described themselves as Ambrosians or Gregorians according as they followed the use of either ordination. The scales, or modes, or tones, belonging to the Roman Church differ essentially from those of the Greeks. The earliest mention of them that has been traced is by our countryman, Alcuin of York, writing under the name of Flaccus Albinus in the latter half of the eighth century, then resident in the court of Charlemagne, whither he had been invited to disseminate English learning through the Gallican Empire. He speaks of there being four authentic and four plagal modes, and of their ordination by authority, probably that of the Pope, and, if so, of Pope Adrian, the Emperor's contemporary. The compulsion of the Roman modes upon Gallican use, which was on grounds of policy and not of art, was among the vexations resisted by the clergy of the latter nation under the rule of Charlemagne. There is reliable evidence that the origin of these Church modes was within the century and a half before the year 800, and St. Gregory and St. Ambrose had no more to do with the same than had St. Peter. The Gallican principles of music were superseded by the Roman, and these again were disturbed by those which are ascribed to Guillaume of Fécamp, whose form of chant was, among other tyrannies of our Norman conquerors, forced upon English adoption in 1083, by Thurstan, Abbot of Glastonbury, previously of Caen in Normandy. There are grounds for supposition, that in the primitive British Church, even before Theodore the Greek, Archbishop of Canterbury, and his companion Adrian were sent hither by Pope Vitalian, to promulgate Romanism in 668, there were a method of chanting and system of music of which some possible relics may still remain, if they cannot be authoritatively proved, in certain of our rural districts. The many fluctuations in the principles of

Church music prior to the time of the Reformation with its enfranchisement of learning, exemplify one constant purpose — the employment of the most advanced condition of the art, from period to period of its progress, the most advanced and the then most modern, in the service of the Sanctuary. They prove also that the system of modes, now fancifully named Gregorian, has had no permanence in this country. Hence, it may be asserted, that those well-meaning men, who would resuscitate the standard use of so-called Gregorian music in the Church of England, evince mistaken zeal, false antiquarianism, illogical deductiveness, artistic blindness, and ecclesiastical error.

Difference of Ecclesiastical from Greek modes.

Originally, the four authentic ecclesiastical modes were named by the odd numbers—first, third, fifth, and seventh; and the four plagal, to make ever obvious their relationship to the others, were named by the even numbers, second, fourth, sixth, and eighth, each pair being thus distinctly coupled. The inverted position of the Tonic and Dominant, as at the interval of a 5th or of a 4th, is so made constantly apparent, for the lower note of each authentic mode is the upper note in the plagal. In the second half of the tenth century, Greek names were adopted[a] for the four authentic modes of the Church, and the Greek prefix *Hypo* marked the four plagal. The most essential difference of principle distinguishes the Ecclesiastical modes from the Greek—namely, that the

---

[a] By Notker.

INTRODUCTORY.   13

latter are all transpositions of the same scale, while the former have each a special arrangement of tones and semitones. To speak precisely, the Ecclesiastical modes are formed each of the notes of our scale of C, each starting, however, from a different degree of the same. In the fifth mode only, now called the Lydian, beginning from F, is it permissible, but yet optional, to employ B, the sole inflected note of the system, and thus to have a perfect 4th from the principal or tonic.

The Dorian is the First Mode, and the Hypo- Dorian. Dorian the second of the Ecclesiastical category. The former has D for its principal note—analogous to the *Tonic* of modern music; and you will observe that this scale, or series of notes in alphabetical succession, has a semitone between its second and third degrees, and between its sixth and seventh, having thus a tone between its seventh and eighth degrees—an effect most unsatisfactory to modern cultivated ears.

A melody in this Dorian mode is employed by Handel as the subject of his fugal chorus in *Israel in Egypt*, "And I will exalt him;"

his motive for employing this peculiar form of melody might more fitly be considered elsewhere than here, but I quote the theme as a not unfamiliar example of the character of the Dorian mode. As another specimen, let me adduce the very early English tune called "Cold and raw," which illustrates a noteworthy fact—namely, that the laity, though, as will presently be shown, they had music distinct from that of the Church, could not but be impressed by what they heard in the chanting of daily prayers, and sometimes consequently framed their secular tunes upon the ecclesiastical scales.

Phrygian. The Third Mode of the Church is the Phrygian and its plagal, the Fourth Mode is the Hypo-Phrygian. The former has E for its principal note, and thus its semitones lie between the first and second, and the fifth and sixth degrees.

Again to quote from Handel's grandest oratorio, the subject of the fugue "Egypt was glad when they departed," also in *Israel in Egypt*, is in the Phrygian mode.

You will mark the singularly plaintive effect of the descent of a semitone to the third bar, which is the striking speciality of this mode, and which is most pertinently exemplified in the choral phrase to the words "Lord, bow thine ear to our pray'r," reiterated with touching pathos throughout the first duet in Mendelssohn's *Elijah*.

The Lydian is the Fifth Mode of Roman use, and the Hypo-Lydian is the sixth. The principal note in the Lydian mode is F; and the semitones lie between the fourth and fifth, and the seventh and eighth degrees.

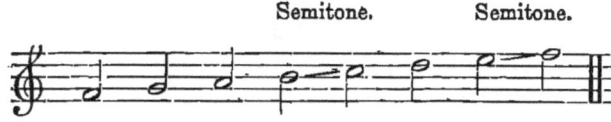

If we may reason from the present to the past, and judge in any degree of the impressions of which Greek ears were susceptible from those which affect our own, we may fairly ascribe the tender character the ancients perceived in this Lydian Mode to the effect of its notes lying within the easy range of a tenor voice, and thence being susceptible of greater sweetness than those of melodies in the Mixo-Lydian, which would exact more force, or than those in the Phrygian and Dorian, which would be given with more and more roughness. The gentler, more acceptable, nay, more musical character of the Church Lydian than of either of the other modes, springs, of course, from its ascent by a semitone to the key-note, which is the form of melodic conclusion that is most satisfactory and most agreeable to us moderns—and which belongs to no other mode than this. Thus there is more of meaning than appears to an unclassical or an unmusical reader, in Dryden's line in "Alexander's Feast "—

"Softly sweet in Lydian measure;"

and it is in the true Greek spirit as much as it is in the pure modern feeling that he assigns this mode of tender expression to the music that lulls the stormy passions of the hero. In Beethoven's quartet in A minor, is a movement which the composer defines as a "Song of gratitude, in the Lydian mode, offered to the Divinity by a convalescent;" the extremely simple theme of this may well show the character of the mode—

INTRODUCTORY. 17

That the charm of this beautiful melody is strangely qualified by the composer's rejection of the discretionary ♭ B of the 5th Mode, must be obvious to all hearers.

The Seventh Mode is the Hyper-Lydian, sometimes called Mixo-Lydian, and the Eighth is the Hypo-Mixo-Lydian; the former dates from the G of modern music, and differs only from our major scale in having a tone instead of a semitone between its chief note and that next below it.

Hyper- or Mixo-Lydian.

* *The same with Beethoven's Harmony.*

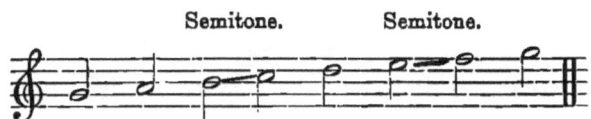

I can call to mind no more familiar example of this mode than the Lutheran Choral, "An Wasserflüssen Babylons," which is characterized by the strain set to the last line but one of the stanza.

* *The same harmonized.*

The examples I have adduced have been sufficient to show that the so-called Gregorian scales are employed sometimes, for special purposes, with good effect by modern composers; and the facts, more than the arguments I have stated, have, I trust, also been sufficient to prove that these scales are wholly unfit—upon historical, artistic, and religious grounds —for standard use in our Church Service. The law of the Reformation, that the Service should be cele-

Roman Church modes inapt to the Church of England.

brated in the vulgar tongue, in order that it might be "understanded of the people," applies as forcibly to the exclusion of the Gregorian chant, as of the Latin words that were originally sung to it in this and other countries of Western Europe.

<small>B flat.</small>   The optional ♭B of the Fifth Mode is of Greek derivation. The middle note of the classic system, whence all intervals were calculated, was the upper A of a bass voice. The Diatonic Tetrachord has its notes at the intervals of a semitone and then two successive tones—

The ♭B of this Tetrachord is the sixth note of the Dorian Mode; but the Hypo-Dorian which counts from the lower A requires ♮B for its second note. Hence, in this pair of Modes the employment of ♭B is limited to the second octave; and the same restriction holds with regard to the discretionary ♭B in the Fifth Mode of Church use. As this was the only inflected note in the music of the mediæval Western Church, a small letter b was employed as its sign; which letter b we still retain, with slight modification of its form, ♭, as the sign of a flat, while the French use the word *bémol* (softened or lowered B) as its name. Further, this flattening of B, and no other note, in early Christendom, accounts for ♭B being the normal note with the Germans, and for the note they brought into use after they had long been familiar with the other seven, being called by them H.

A B C D   E F G A   H C D E

We now come to the consideration of harmony — *Harmony originated by the Northern laity.* the combination of musical sounds—which is not of Southern nor of ecclesiastical origin, but purely a discovery of Northern nations, who attained to a rude maturity in its practice with no guidance but that of their natural instinct. Many proofs that our Saxon and Danish ancestors had the habit of singing in parts—from the writings of Giraldus Cambrensis (Gerald Barry) and other early authorities—have been brought to modern light by Mr. W. Chappell, in his researches into the nationality of music in England; but one proof in particular of this interesting fact has been rendered widely familiar by the Rev. C. Kingsley's[a] picturesque romance of *Hereward*, wherein an incident which strikingly bears upon it is quoted, nay, the very words introduced, from an ancient Latin version of the cotemporaneous Anglo-Saxon chronicle of the deeds of the last opponent of our Norman invaders. Hereward and two companions, the story runs, disguised themselves as minstrels, in order to gain admission to a marriage feast in the castle of the King of Cornwall; and to maintain their

---

[a] Afterwards Canon Kingsley of Westminster.

assumed character they sang, sometimes separately and sometimes according to the manner of the Gervians, together in three parts. These Gervians were the residents of our Eastern counties, and Hereward himself—a native of Bourne, in Lincolnshire—was familiarly versed in all the arts, civil as well as military, of his compatriots. An evidence of the continued popularity of this national manner of singing in harmony of three parts, appears in the Freemen's Songs of the time of Henry VIII., some specimens of which—" Of all the birds," and " We be three poor mariners," for instance—were printed in Ravenscroft's *Deuteromelia* in 1609, and frequent mention of them occurs in writings of a century earlier, indifferently as Freemen's or as Threemen's Songs. To pass forward to our own time, I am assured by several persons who have lived among the country folk of Essex, that these still sing, at harvest feasts, at Christmas, and on other social occasions, appropriate songs in three-part harmony which have probably never been written, the singers having no technical knowledge of music. I have other personal testimony that the faculty of what may be called natural harmony is not more general on the east than on the west side of our island, since in Wales the peasantry may commonly be heard singing unwritten three-part music. Let me not arrogate, however, that the origination of multi-part music belongs alone to this country, or either of the nations that have peopled it; the Rev. Professor Sir F. A. G. Ouseley has shown that the untaught practice of extempore part singing prevails among the Russian peasantry, and there is plentiful authority for the assertion that this exists in all Northern lands and has existed since the utmost range of man's memory or his records. Let me take a step higher in the social scale, and turn from the wholly untutored rustics to those of the community who enjoyed general, though not musical, or at least not harmonic, education; and among these we shall not rarely find persons with a miniature celebrity for singing what they call "Second"—that is, for improvising an under part to a known melody upon the suggestion of their natural sense of euphony. Mankind, in the south of Europe, appears to be endowed with such facility in melodizing, that the people may be said to make their cantilenas in the very act of singing them, and thus, having the habit of constantly producing new variations of certain routine progressions, they have no memory for the airs of other than their own times, and possess in consequence scarcely a national melody of two generations old; we of the North, on the contrary, if our tunes are less easily wrought, seem to work in more enduring material, since we have produced tuneful crystals that have been treasured in the traditions and archives of our nations for ages, and as if in compensation for our want of the Southern melodic fluency, we possess, gentle and simple, the inborn faculty of enriching our tunes with harmonic combination. Herein we find a phase of the imaginative character of those races who see in their mist-clad trees and rocks, and mountain peaks, something besides their substance, who fancifully people the elements with a host of fairy existences, and whose musical conceptions are not the bare outline of superficial certainty without the investiture of such under-current of thought as quickens fact into poetry.

Having thus far considered the historical origin of harmony, let me assume that the endeavour is worthy of this truth-seeking age, to attempt the exposition of the arbitrary laws that long regulated its use, and the natural principles that have in some degree superseded them, to those who study music from a pleasurable rather than a professional point of view.

Key. In modern music, all coherence, both of melody and of harmony, all relationship, all principle, is involved in the arrangement of notes which constitutes a Key. This arrangement refers to any note that may be arbitrarily chosen as the key-note. The key-note is in a piece of music, to speak comparatively, as the point of sight is in a perspective drawing, whence all the lines diverge, and which regulates the proportions of all the objects in the picture. There are two kinds of key, major and minor; each of which has seven diatonic notes and five chromatic, whose total is the twelve sounds already noticed as comprised in an octave; and the names of these, and their inflection by sharps or flats, depend upon their relation to the key-note.

Major. In a major key, the diatonic notes stand at the intervals from the key-note of major 2nd, major 3rd, perfect 4th, perfect 5th, major 6th, major 7th, and perfect 8th—which last is a repetition of the first, being the beginning of a second octave.

The 6th degree of the major key is the key-note of **Minor.** a minor key, which, unfortunately, is called its relative minor; and the 3rd degree of this minor key is consequently the relative major; thus C and A, D and B, ♭E and C, are relatives major and minor. The relationship of these keys consists in there being more notes in common between them than there are between a major key and any other minor key than its so-called relative; and the relationship is indicated by the two keys having the same signature. There is some analogy to the Ecclesiastical system in the frequent use of the term *mode* when speaking of these qualities of major or minor in a key; it is a remnant indeed of the Church theory to regard the major mode and its relative minor mode as modifications of the same scale—a theory which is opposed to natural truth, and which has consequently sometimes induced harmonic obscurity in compositions even of the greatest masters. There is an important distinction between a major key and its relative minor, in the employment in the minor of an accidental sharp or natural to raise its 7th degree to the interval of a semitone below the key-note; and the observance of this prevents confusion between any relative major and minor keys. The notes in a minor key that differ from those of the major key of the same keynote are the 3rd and 6th, which are minor instead of major.

It must be understood, then, that the variations of major and minor are modifications of the *one same key*, not of the *two relative keys*, and it will be seen that a minor key has either three flats more for its signature than the major key of the same key-note;

or, that a major key has three sharps more than the minor.

This term, relative, is here regretfully used in application to two keys that are totally distinct, not only in æsthetical effect, but in natural derivation; regretfully, because it has led to many a most evil misapprehension, and because it is a stumbling-block in the way of learners. I should rejoice to cast it away, now and for ever, but fear that a thing so deeply rooted in general acceptance as is this will not yield to a cast; I aim, however, to explain it away, hoping by reason more than violence to weaken its misleading power. Every note of the key of C minor is differently derived, and differently treated, and differently felt, from the same notes in the key of ♭ E, and this truth must be for ever present in the thought of the melodist and the harmonist.

There will arise constant occasion for mention of the several degrees of the diatonic scale by their general tonal, not their particular alphabetical names, which therefore I will state and explain :— <small>Names of the 7 notes of a key.</small>

The note from which a key is named, and from which the intervals or distances of all the other notes are measured, is called indifferently the key-note or the Tonic.

The note of next importance to this, is the 5th degree of the scale; which, because it commands or determines the key, is called the Dominant. The note C, even with the chord that naturally springs from it, might belong to several different keys;

but the note G, the 5th of C, so satisfactorily dominates over it as strongly to define its tonality.

The 4th of a key is called the Subdominant. There are two reasons for this name; 1st, because it stands one degree in the scale *under* the dominant; 2nd, that it stands at the same interval from the tonic downwards, that the dominant does upwards,

and is thus the *under* dominant. The subdominant further justifies its name by the manner in which it also affects the key; for, as the dominant chord proves that a key has not one flat more, or one sharp less, than its due number,

so the subdominant chord shows that it has not a sharp more, or a flat less, than belongs to it.

The note which stands next *above* the tonic—the 2nd of the key, is therefore named the Supertonic.

The 3rd of the key, because it stands midway between the tonic and the dominant, is named the Mediant.

The Submediant is the 6th of the key, and takes its name from standing in the same position between the tonic and subdominant downwards, that the mediant holds between the tonic and dominant upwards.

The 7th of the key, the Leading note, takes its name from the necessity of its rising or *leading* to the key-note in a full close.

From its peculiarly keen effect in certain harmonic combinations, as much as its seeming eagerness to ascend to its adjacent tonic, this 7th of the key is also frequently called the Sensitive-note. The perception of the delicate and very individual character of this note is however entirely a development of modern times, the early harmonists, even those who wrote till the middle of the eighteenth century—I may instance Handel and Bach as at once the brightest and the most accessible examples—having shown themselves utterly regardless of that prominent peculiarity which is most obvious to a modern cultivated ear.

The scale of C shows the gradual relation of the several notes, with their distinctive names;

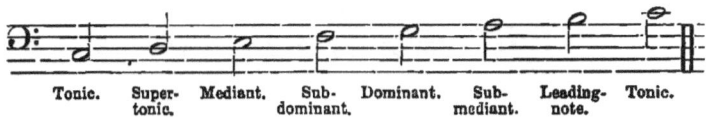

Tonic.   Super-tonic.   Mediant.   Sub-dominant.   Dominant.   Sub-mediant.   Leading-note.   Tonic.

and the corresponding degrees of every other key bear the same names in reference to their tonic that those in the scale here presented bear to its tonic C; thus A is the dominant of D, ♭B is the dominant of ♭E, and the like.

Close, Cadence, or Fall.

I have alluded to the progression of the leading note in a full close. Let me define this term, close, as meaning the completion of any rhythmical period. Its synonym, cadence, is quite as often used in the same simple sense; but, as the practice has become common for the performer to insert a flourish at a close or cadence, we conventionally use the word cadence, to denote the flourish introduced at a close. Our elder writers often employ the word, fall—which has the same etymological meaning—in the same technical sense as cadence; thus, in *Twelfth Night*, the Duke commands "That strain again, it had a dying *fall*," by which he means that the melody died away at its final close or cadence.

A Full Close, or Perfect Cadence, is almost unexceptionally in modern music, when a passage terminates on the chord of the tonic preceded by that of the dominant; <small>Full Close,</small>

and in this, strangely as our revered elders ignored the peculiarity, the cultivated ear now demands that the leading-note rise by a semitone to the tonic. Another form of full close—which is all but obsolete, or, at least, most rarely employed in the music of our day save where this is intended to suggest associations of the past—is when the chord of the tonic is preceded by that of the subdominant at the termination of a period.

32   *INTRODUCTORY.*

This latter is called the **Plagal Cadence,** the other being received as the **Authentic**—terms, be it remembered, that denote respectively the interval of a 4th or of a 5th.

Half Close.   A Half Close is when a passage ends upon the chord of the dominant, regardless of what harmony may precede it.

Interrupted Close.   An Interrupted Close is when a passage has seemed to approach a perfect cadence, and this is broken off by some chord other than that of the expected tonic.

Here is a strain of music comprising a half, an interrupted, and a full close, each rhythmical period in which contains two bars, and the special character of the several forms of cadence is to be observed in the distinctive effect of each.

It is now needful to define the difference between a concord and a discord. In so doing, all the beautiful poetic distinctions must be ignored which teach us to shrink with horror from the one, and to look for infinite loveliness in the other. The term concord indeed implies, in its most limited technical sense, repose; but this would be such as repose in a polar desert, under the unvarying gaze of a six months' sun, from a naked sky unadorned with a cloud, and with no tree or shrub or sign of life around to break the changeless, colourless, soundless stillness. Dissonance is as essential to musical beauty as is any variation of a straight line to interest in the pictorial arts; and it is chiefly in the progression from discord to concord that the true charm of this latter is felt.

Concord and Discord

A Concord is when two or more musical sounds in combination are satisfactory in themselves, and can form therefore the conclusion, or point of repose, of any passage.

A Discord is when two notes are unsatisfactory in their effect until they are followed by some particular harmony, their progression to which constitutes the *resolution* of the discord.

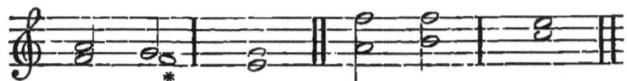

A discord, therefore, can never be conclusive, since, however prolonged, it must finally be resolved; and it is thus the musical exponent of unrest, activity, aspiration.

Philosophy takes the place of poetry in affording an illustration of the distinction between concord and discord, more beautiful perhaps than any metaphor. It is this: the vibrations of the air inducing musical sounds, by a process which might be called phonography, imprint their undulations by causing lightly scattered sand to gather together in the shapes of their curves; when the sounds are consonant, these curves take what plastic artists teach us are the forms of beauty; when they are dissonant, the curves are distorted, jagged, harsh to the eye, as is to the ear the musical combination that induces them. Again, if less striking, another acoustical phenomenon is not less pertinent—namely, vibrations are more or less rapid in proportion as the sound is higher or lower of which they are the utterance, and combinations are more or less consonant in proportion to the greater or less number of coincident vibrations of the two sounds —thus, two sounds in unison (the most complete consonants) vibrate simultaneously; the upper note of an 8th has two vibrations for every one of the lower; while the minor 2nd (one of the harshest discords) has sixteen vibrations of its upper note for every fifteen of its lower, the coincidences of which vibrations are as rare as the dissonance of the combination is obvious.

You will please to regard this morning's discourse as introductory, and allow me to hope in subsequent lectures to interest you with practical applications of what has been now explained.

LECTURE II.

THE ANCIENT STRICT OR DIATONIC STYLE.

UNDERSTANDING as we now do the distinctions of the diatonic and chromatic genera of the Greeks, it is time to consider the application of these terms as definitions of two broad styles in music. We must pause, however, on the threshold of this examination to note some of the landmarks in musical history, in order to ascertain the sources of these two styles, and thence trace their diversity.

The eighth century or, at earliest, the close of the seventh, saw the institution of a system of music for ecclesiastical use that may have had its origin in Greek precedent, but essentially differs from that in principle and effect. The Church system comprises a series of scales which are antipathetic to modern ears, because they are at variance with the tonal system that modern times have developed. Rome sent her missionaries through Gaul hither, the field of whose teaching was by degrees extended into the countries of the north-east; and wherever they carried the Christian religion they carried with it the Church scales as the vehicle for utterance of the prayers. In this country and throughout the native land of the Teuton, they found the practice among the people of singing their popular or national songs in harmony. Appropriating this barbaric practice, and engrafting it upon the musical system, which as yet acknowledged but unisonous singing, the Church then admitted the performance of descant, or accompanying melody, together with the Cantus Fermus—Canto Fermo—Plain Song. This descant consisted of such notes as were prompted by the euphonious instinct of the singers, and was always extemporaneous, as was the popular harmony of the laity. In course of time rules were framed to direct its construction, and, when it came to be written instead of improvised, it took the name of Counterpoint, denoting that it was sung *against* the point or theme. At first, descant or counterpoint was in notes of equal length to those of the subject; in this form of note against note it is called Plain or simple Counterpoint. Subsequently, various figurative forms were introduced, all of which—having notes of less or greater length than those of the subject—are comprised in the term Florid Counterpoint, and in this occur the three classes of diatonic discord presently to be described. The plain song of the Church being always in one or other of the modes, necessitated corresponding modal restrictions in the counterpoint constructed upon it; and, as the modal arrangement of the succession of sounds was entirely arbitrary, so were the laws that regulated their combination similarly artificial. These were wholly regardless of the phenomenon since discovered of the generation of harmonic sounds by a fundamental note or root; and they refer therefore to the several combinations of intervals as each a separate fact, without any general principle or bond of unity. As time advanced, the number of the modes was enlarged. There was added to those in Church use the Æolian, commencing on A, which is identical with the Æolian of Pindar, and is the single one of the Greek modes that appears intact in the Church system. Under the name of relative minor to the major tonic of a 3rd above, this mode has perplexed, more than all the rest of the cumbrous antique machinery, the progress of natural music. At last, under the name of the Ionian mode, our modern scale of C—with the semitones standing between its 3rd and 4th, and between its 7th and 8th degrees—was included in the ecclesiastical system, though it was despised by the orthodox, the art conservatives of those days, as a lascivious innovation. Consequent upon this, but at first by very slow gradations, the natural harmonic system took its rise; but its progress was long retarded, nay, it is still in some degree embarrassed, by the conventional restraints of the earlier style. Modern theorists have codified the laws of counterpoint, and reduced them to such systematic order that they may be mastered by every student; and, submitting to these laws, modern writers have produced and always may produce compositions in the elder style, strikingly distinct in character from those expressed in the natural idiom of their own age. Occasions arise for the appropriate momentary assumption of the manner of former centuries—such as the wish to give special gravity to a particular piece, or to invest it with mediæval associations; and, in order to appreciate music written with this design, and to estimate the antique compositions which it emulates, the modern student should master the laws of counterpoint and so approach the fundamental or massive harmonic school by the path of history.

There is perfect analogy between these ancient and modern styles in music, and firstly, the Hieratic or Archaic style in Greek sculpture and that of Phidias and Praxiteles; and secondly, the style of the first Christian painters and that of Raffaelle and his followers. The former, in all three cases, is conventional, limited, and, so to speak, dogmatic; the latter is, in every respect of subject and treatment, natural and free. Ancient and Modern Styles.

The word Diatonic—rendered *through the tones* by etymologists—must have been intended to signify *through the uninflected notes*, as opposed to Chromatic, which referred to an accidental sharp in every tetrachord; *tonos*, in this case, signifying tone or sound, and not an interval of two semitones. When it was rediscovered that any arrangement of notes might be reproduced in a higher or lower pitch by the insertion of sharps or flats to adjust the position of the semitones, it was found that the diatonic principle of non-inflected notes was preserved, though a piece of music were transposed one or more notes higher or lower, and the sharps or flats essential to the new key were employed. The next step was the discovery of modulation, that is, the art of passing from one key to another in the course of the same piece; and this also is true to the diatonic principles, since the sharps or flats that mark the new key belong to its natural and uninflected scale. Progressing further, musicians observed the satisfactory effect of rising to the tonic by a semitone rather than a tone, and the accidental that marks the leading note in a minor key then became incorporated in the diatonic style. A signal result of the inclination, nay, the demand of the natural ear for the fine delicate interval of a semitone between the leading note and the tonic, instead of the gross rough major 2nd that lies between the 7th and 8th degrees of most of the Church modes, is that, in melodies preserved by oral tradition, this note is always altered from what we find in early written copies of the same tunes; as one among numberless examples of what I say, let me instance "John Anderson, my Jo," which air, according to its Æolian mode, closes in old copies with the ascent of a whole tone to the key-note,

But blessings on your fros-ty pow, John An-der-son, my Jo.

but is now universally sung and universally printed with the change of this to a semitone,

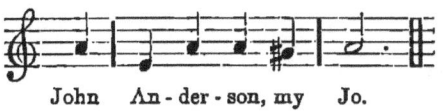
John An - der - son, my Jo.

which proves that, on natural grounds, this major 7th is a necessary interval of the minor key.

Having defined the word diatonic, let us now look into the peculiarities of the style it designates. The ancient style may be described as contrapuntal, because in it each part of the harmony is an independent melody, sometimes woven round a fixed theme, or, in the absence of this, sometimes forming the theme or basis of another melodious woof, so that every part is in fact a counterpoint to all the others; whereas, the modern style may be better represented by the word fundamental or generative, since its harmonies are referable to certain roots—fundamental or generative notes—from which they are traced upwards in masses, instead of running side by side in continuous lines. The following are examples of plain and florid counterpoint.

ISRAEL IN EGYPT.—*Handel.*

And be-liev-ed the Lord and his ser-vant Mo-ses.

MESSIAH.—*Handel.*

And with his stripes we are heal-ed.

The following is an example of complete chords, dispersed in arpeggio, supporting a melody which is dependent upon them.

ELIJAH.—*Mendelssohn.*

If with all your hearts ye truly seek him.

The ancient or contrapuntal style may also be described as strict or uniform, because its rules are invariable; whereas the modern fundamental style may be represented as free, since, in it, certain notes of a key bear a treatment widely exceptional from the strict rules that still govern the rest of the scale. Too much stress cannot be laid on this unexceptional treatment of every note of the diatonic style; as however there will be frequent need of recurrence to its mention, I will now only state that, whatever progressions or combinations within the key are admissible for any one note of the scale, are available for every note; and that, whatever is unallowable for all the notes, is, of course, forbidden for each particular one.*

The ancient, contrapuntal, or strict style, may further be designated diatonic, because no notes are employed in it that belong not to the diatonic scale of the key, major or minor, which for the time may prevail; whereas, the modern, or fundamental, or free style is chromatic, not because all its passages must necessarily proceed by semitones, but because in it accidentals may be used that induce no change of key. Modern composers who, for some special dramatic, illustrative, or associative purpose, occasionally adopt the diatonic style, for the most part pay such deference to modern ears as to satisfy them with either the authentic or the plagal form of a perfect cadence, which by reason of its early establishment as a requirement of good effect, may be regarded as the link between the ancient and the modern styles.

The concords in the diatonic style are, I., the perfect unison, 5th and 8th, called perfect because their expansion or contraction by the sharpening or flattening of either of the notes changes them from concords into discords; *Diatonic Concords.*

---

* See "Tritone," "Leading note," "Mediant," pages 45 and 46.

and II., the major and minor 3rds, and their inversions, the minor and major 6ths, which are not perfect but flexible, since they can be taken with equally consonant effect in either of these forms of major or minor.

Common Chords. The combination of any bass note with its perfect 5th and either major or minor 3rd constitutes a common chord, which is named either major or minor according to the quality of its 3rd.

You will observe in this last example that the variation of the flexible 3rd substitutes one concord for another, both of which are equally agreeable to the ear, since reposeful or conclusive in their effect. You will observe in the next example that the alteration of the perfect 5th, either by augmentation or diminution, changes the harmony from a concord to a discord, harsh in its sound, and requiring resolution upon the succeeding concord.

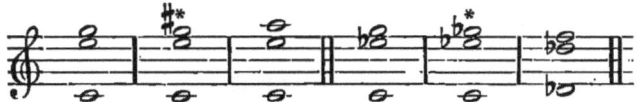

Either or all of the three notes of a common chord may be doubled in the unison or the octave, which doubled note is no new element of the harmony, but simply an enrichment of the body of sound produced without it.

The progression from the subdominant to the leading note in a major key is by three degrees of whole tones, and the interval is named therefore the Tritone. *Tritone.*

Tone. Tone. Tone.   Tritone.

The leap of an augmented 4th, from one to the other of the extreme notes of a tritone, is objectionable in melody; and our repugnance to it results from the two notes being characteristic of different keys—the

F suggesting to the ear, in the following example, a key that contains ♭B,

and the B leading us to expect, in the following, a key that contains ♯ F.

The inversion of this interval of the augmented 4th, by placing the subdominant above the leading note, produces that of the diminished 5th.

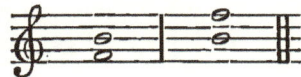

Triad of the Leading note. It is essential to a common chord that the 5th be perfect; hence it is no exception from the uniformity of the diatonic style, that it allows no common chord upon the leading note, since, by the constitution of the diatonic scale, it contains not the notes to constitute a common chord upon its 7th degree.

Triad of the Mediant. In a major key, the common chord of the mediant can scarcely be employed without involving such juxtaposition of the extreme notes of the tritone as produces a harsh effect; and therefore, though this chord is sometimes to be found in ancient music, good taste can scarcely accept it as a concord. The system, I believe first practised by Sebastian Bach, which has now become general, of tuning keyed instruments by equal temperament, consists in prevaricating the enharmonic diesis—the distinction, that is, between ♯D and ♭E, &c.—by tuning notes too sharp for the one and too flat for the other of their names, and by making a like compromise between the still minuter discrepancies of the diatonic scale, so that, while no interval is perfectly true, the ear is in neither case shocked by false intonation. It is however a beautiful and a wonderful property of the musical sense, so to adjust these tempered notes that, in every key, they produce the same effect upon us in relation to other notes, that the perfectly tuned notes would produce which they represent. I shall have to revert to this phenomenon, but I must here illustrate it by the fact that the chord of E minor—which sounds strange and foreign when taken in the key of C—sounds familiar and natural when taken in any key containing ♯F, in whose scale the notes of this chord occur,

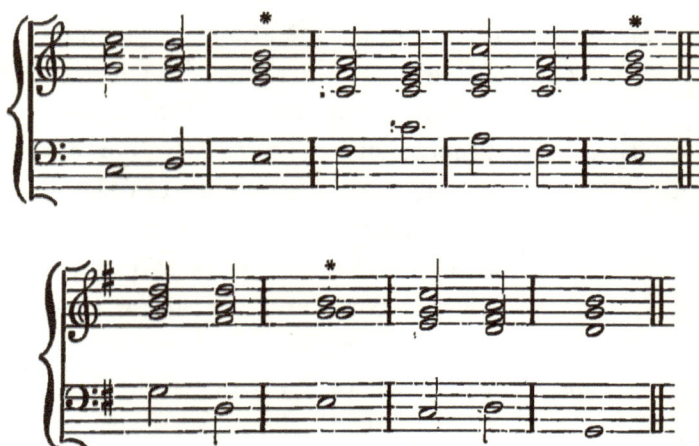

48   THE ANCIENT STRICT OR DIATONIC STYLE.

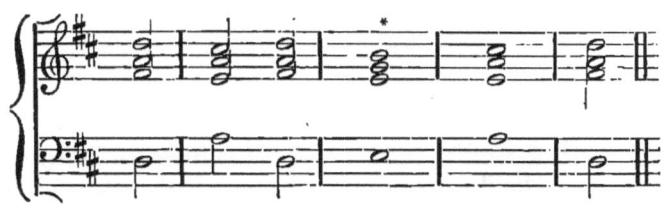

whence it is obvious, that we feel something different in the same combination of these self-same notes, as represented by the pianoforte key-board, when taken in relation to one or another key-note.

Common Chords in major keys.   Granting that the rules against the use of the tritone exclude, in most cases, the chord of the mediant as a dissonance—so that its unavailability is no exception from, but a fulfilment of, the diatonic law—there are five common chords in a major key; of which those of the tonic, subdominant, and dominant are major; and those of the supertonic and submediant are minor.

Major. Minor. Major. Minor. Major.

Triads of Supertonic and Mediant in minor keys.   The alteration of the 3rd and 6th degrees of a minor key from major into minor, changes the quality of all the chords in which either of these notes appears. The minor 6th of the key—less by a semitone than a major 6th—is of course but a diminished 5th above the supertonic;

hence, in a minor key the supertonic, for the same reason as the leading note, bears no common chord. Again, the minor 3rd—less by a semitone than the major 3rd—stands at the interval of an augmented 5th below the leading note;

hence—without entering on the ground, debated by some theorists, of the relative dissonance of the mediant chord in a major key—the mediant with its 3rd and 5th in a minor key is positively dissonant, irrespective of all relationship to other sounds.

There are then but four common chords in a minor key; of which the tonic and subdominant are minor —instead of major as in a major key; the submediant is major—instead of minor as in a major key; and the dominant, the only common chord containing neither the 3rd nor 6th of the key, is the same major chord that we have in the major key.

Common Chords in minor keys.

Minor. Major. Minor. Major.

Dominant and Submediant in minor keys.

The two contiguous major chords of the dominant and submediant, standing at the interval of a semitone from one another, are unlike in their character—the one being as soft, rich, and tender in its effect, as the other is bright and vigorous. The direct progression from either of these to its neighbour, forcibly brings out the speciality of the other chord; and indeed, very much of the pathos and of the rough energy of expression ascribed to the minor key, often springs from some particular employment of the latter or former of these chords.

Tonic major chord.

One other common chord, however, is also employed in the diatonic style, of which moreover it is strongly characteristic, although it cannot be written without an accidental. This is the major chord of the tonic in a minor key, which was universally employed in final closes by early writers, and was written as frequently at least as the minor chord by composers as late as

THE ANCIENT STRICT OR DIATONIC STYLE. 51

the middle of the last century, but rarely appears in modern music save where an imitation is designed of that sudden but solemn effect peculiar to the older style.

The inversion of a chord is the placing one of its other notes, instead of the root, in the bass. The only inversion of a common chord available in the diatonic style, is when the 3rd stands as the bass note, the root being at the interval of a 6th above this, and the 5th of the original chord being at the interval of a 3rd above the bass.

Inversion of concords.

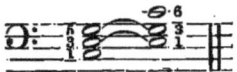

Though the inversion of a chord contain no other notes than the chord in its direct form, and differ from this only in the position of these notes with regard to each other, the effect of the combination is greatly changed by the alteration of its form. Compare, for instance, the solid, firm, determinate character of a direct chord—one, namely, having its root in the bass, with the lighter, brighter perhaps, and gentler effect of the same chord inverted—that is, having its 3rd in the bass.

E 2

52   THE ANCIENT STRICT OR DIATONIC STYLE.

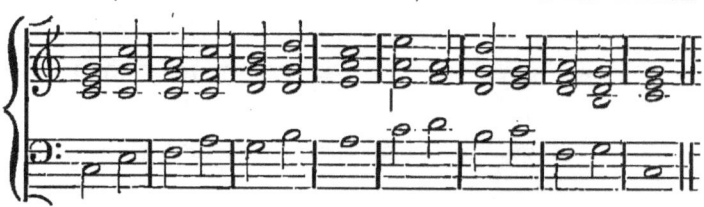

Inversion of diminished triad.
A still more remarkable change of effect is induced by the inversion of the chord containing a diminished 5th; for, the grating dissonance of this interval is so far smoothed by placing the intermediate third below it,

that in this inverted form it is classed among the concords of the ancient style. Yet further, this inverted chord with the diminished 5th was often written by early composers in preference to the dominant harmony, as the penultimate chord in a

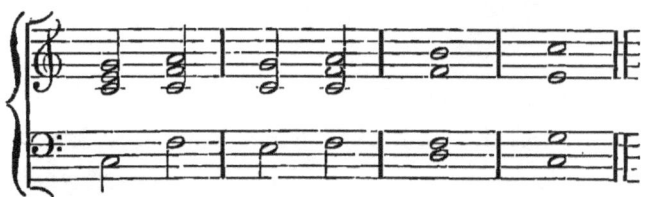

full close; the reasons for the satisfactory effect of which, will be best explained when the true fundamental origin of the chord has been discussed.

One more instance of the change of the effect of a chord that is induced by inversion is in the triad of the mediant, the discordance of which is dispelled even more obviously than that of the diminished triad, when its 3rd is sounded as the bass.

Every note af a major key may then be taken as the bass of an inverted concord, and we may thus have the consecutive notes of the scale with an inversion on each, or we may intermix inversions with chords in the original position. The 3rd and 7th of the key, however, can only be taken in the bass when bearing an inversion.

The augmented 5th, which stands between the mediant and the leading note in a minor key, is always dissonant, in whatever position it occurs, whether direct or inverted.

Inversion of concords in minor keys.

The dominant of a minor key cannot therefore stand as the bass of a complete inverted concord, but it may be accompanied with its 6th only.

54 THE ANCIENT STRICT OR DIATONIC STYLE.

The minor scale thus presents the following series of inverted concords.

Inversion on minor 7th. To avoid the unmelodious effect of the augmented 2nd between the 7th and 6th degreess of the minor scale, it is admissible, when the bass descends gradually from the tonic to the submediant, to employ the minor 7th, as the bass of an inverted concord;

and we thus obtain harmony for the entire scale of the Æolian mode, which must however be used with careful discretion, to avoid confusion between the relative minor and major keys, as in the following passage, where the seventh chord indicates the key of E flat, which key, however, is not satisfactorily confirmed before the resumption of the original key of C minor.

Such confusion is at times to be found in music of admirable composers; but it is to warn less gifted writers against emulating their defects instead of their beauties, rather than to carp at the occasional irregularities of masters in the art, that this admission is made.

Examples of music in plain counterpoint, consisting almost exclusively of concords, are to be found in the early harmony of Psalm-tunes and in the church music of Tallis, Farrant, and their cotemporaries; and, of a gayer character, in the Villanellas of Naples and Venice, and their English representatives, the Songs of four parts, Ballets, or Fal-las, of the end of the sixteenth, and beginning of the seventeenth centuries.[a]

---

[a] The indecision of key that is frequent in compositions of the period, a fruit of the then remaining prevalence of the Ecclesiastical modes, makes it often doubtful whether a chord be the mediant of one key or the sub-mediant of another; but it is rare, if ever, that the context presents the semitone above the bass of that chord in such proximity as to induce the false relation of the tritone.

THE ANCIENT STRICT OR DIATONIC STYLE.

Pedals.

A Pedal is a bass note continued through several chords, of which, indifferently, it either is or is not a portion.

The pedal in harmony probably takes its name from the pedals of the organ, one of which may be easily held down by the foot, while the hands play the progression of chords on the manual key-board; it may also have been called pedal, from its being the foot or basis of the entire musical structure.

The ancient style anticipates, in some degree, the modern, not only in the special treatment of chords in the several closes or cadences, but in the distinctive character allowed to the dominant and the tonic in their being the only notes that can be employed as pedals.

A dominant pedal produces the effect of climax, leading us from chord to chord more and more to desire, more and more to expect the close to which it must lead. A tonic pedal, on the contrary, has the effect of confirming the conclusion indicated by a perfect cadence, and expresses satisfaction or rest, as opposed to the sense of progress conveyed by a dominant pedal. The following illustrates the different characters of the two.

THE ANCIENT STRICT OR DIATONIC STYLE. 57

FUGUE 4.—*Bach's* 48 Preludes and Fugues.

[musical score with Dominant pedal and Tonic Pedal markings]

A Sequence, in the strict style, is the repetition of a melodic or harmonic progression at a higher or lower part of the scale, without a change of key. The following is the melodic progression of a 4th, with a sequence of two repetitions, each being a note higher than the preceding progression.

Sequences.

The following is the same progression with a common chord on each note.

Observe that in each of the parts, as in the bass, the succession of notes in each repetition is the same as in the original progression; with this exception, that while the intervals have all the same names—as 2nd, 3rd, &c.—their quality is changed by the circumstances of the scale; thus, the part next to the bass proceeds a minor 3rd, from C to A, in the original progression—and again a minor 3rd, from D to B, in the first repetition—but it proceeds a major 3rd, from E to C in the second repetition. In like manner, the quality of the chords changes at each repetition; thus, in the original progression, both chords are major—in the first repetition, the first chord is minor and the second major—and in the second repetition, both chords are minor.

It has been seen that, in melody, the leap of an augmented 4th is repugnant to the ear; and small experience will prove that its vocal intonation is as difficult as its effect is unmelodious. When taken as one of the repetitions in a sequence, however, its resemblance to the perfect 4th of the original progression is sufficient to balance its peculiarity, and thus divesting it of its cacophonous effect, to render it comparatively easy of execution and acceptable to the ear. A passage in which the augmented 4th occurs incidentally will prove the normal melodic character of this interval;

and a prolongation of our former melodic sequence will show how its practicability and its acceptability are modified by its likeness to, though not identity with, the preceding progression.

In like manner, the imperfect chords, which have been shown to be unavailable as concords, may be used in the repetitions of a passage in sequence, in the place of the perfect chords that have the corresponding position in the original progression, their analogy to which sufficiently dissipates their harshness to prevent their disturbing the consonant character of a passage.

Notwithstanding this remarkable licence of progression and combination in the repetitions of a sequence, that would be intolerable in an isolated passage—a licence which the law grants and the ear approves—diatonic composers had generally a strong disinclination to the sound of the augmented 4th in melody, and the diminished 5th to the bass in harmony; to evade this, therefore, when the interval presented itself in the repetition of a sequence, they would frequently render both the 4th and the 5th perfect, by flattening the 7th of the scale.

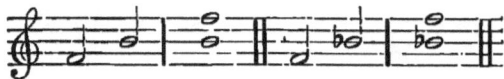

Here then is another note that can only be indicated by an accidental, but yet may not be accounted chromatic, since its use in this particular sense is peculiar to the diatonic style and very common among diatonic writers. From their employment, indeed, of this common chord on the minor 7th of the key, spring many of the quaint effects which strike the general hearer as specially typical of the old composers, of which I cannot better remind you than by quoting a bold and most emphatic passage in sequence from the chorus of "The horse and his rider," in *Israel in Egypt.*

THE ANCIENT STRICT OR DIATONIC STYLE. 61

Discords, you will remember, differ from concords in their necessity to be resolved each on a particular note, whereas concords are unrestricted in their progression. The discords in the diatonic style are the 4th from the bass, any diminished or augmented interval from the bass, the augmented 5th or diminished 4th from any part in the harmony, and any two notes next each other in alphabetical order.

Diatonic discords.

Discords are either Passing-notes, or Suspensions, or Essential Discords; each of which classes requires separate examination.

Passing-notes are notes which belong not to chords. They fill up what would else be a leap from one to another note of the same chord, or from a note of one chord to a note of another chord.

Passing-notes.

They are taken also between the repetitions of one note, whether this belong always to one chord, or the harmony change with each of its repetitions.

Were it not for the employment of passing-notes, all music would have the gravity of psalm-tunes, or, where this was out of keeping, the cumbrous stiffness that would usurp its place. All lightness, all grace, all freedom in melody result from a judicious use of passing-notes; this was the earliest deviation from the primitive form of plain or simple counterpoint in note against note; and its introduction is ascribed, by theorists and historians of the age next after his own, to John of Dunstable, who lived in the first half of the fifteenth century, and who left many proofs of his musical knowledge and attainments in general science.

Arbitrary alterations of minor scale. To avoid the unmelodious interval of the augmented 2nd, in florid passages in minor keys, two arbitrary alterations of the scale are commonly made in the case of passing-notes. The major 6th fills up the interval between the dominant and the leading note;

the minor 7th fills up that between the submediant and the key note.

A scale, in a minor key, running through the entire octave, may thus have the major 6th and the major 7th if ascending—because it is desirable to rise to the key-note by a semitone ; and it may have the minor 7th and minor 6th if descending—because it is also desirable to fall to the dominant by a semitone.

Neither of these passages, however, would be satisfactory if not accompanied by a chord that determined the key, which is rendered equivocal by the confusion of the notes of the minor and major keys in the variations of the scale.

Passing-notes may occur simultaneously in several parts; provided that the parts which move, while others sustain against them, proceed always harmoniously with each other.

Double passing-notes.

Leap of 3rd. The strict rule for passing-notes in the ancient style is, that they must always be approached and quitted by the step of a 2nd, and that they must always occur at a less accented part of the measure than the harmony note from which they proceed, as has been shown in the foregoing examples. Very important exceptions from this characterize the use of passing-notes in modern music, of which it will be fitting to speak at length when other distinctions of this style are explained. It is needful here, however, to call attention to a seeming exception from the rule in the diatonic style, and to show that, instead of an exception, this is truly a confirmation of the law. A passing-note, instead of passing directly to the note next above or below it, may leap the interval of a 3rd to the note beyond this, and then return to the note within such 3rd; this last note in a group of four is the resolution of the passing-note which is the second of the group, the intervening note being a florid ornamentation.

The melodic figure formed by this treatment of passing-notes is of very common occurrence in the florid divisions of the bravura music of the former part of the last century;* the songs of Handel, Hasse, Graun, and their Italian fellow-labourers, abound in such. It assumes a stronger importance in some modern melodies, of which it forms not the mere embellishment, but the characteristic feature; as for instance—

L'ITALIANA IN ALGIERI.—*Rossini.*

ANNA BOLENA.—*Donizetti.*

LUCREZIA BORGIA.—*Donizetti.*

Suspension is retaining a note which has been sounded either singly or as part of the preceding harmony, while a chord is struck of which it forms no essential part. The previous sounding of the note which is to become a discord, is called its *preparation;* the *resolution* of a suspension is its proceeding to a note

Suspensions.

---

* The group is technically styled "changing-notes"

of the chord against which it forms a dissonance, this chord always continuing until the suspension be resolved, albeit sometimes one or more of the parts may move from one to another interval of this same chord.

To speak in more homely terms, suspension is when one part in a progression of harmony proceeds after instead of with the others, and thus virtually lags a step behind the march of its comrades; this you will perceive if you compare the last with the following example, wherein the suspended discords are averted, by making the essential notes of the harmony come altogether.

The suspended discords are the 9th, and the 4th, and also the 5th, from the mediant and leading-note.

Suspended 9th.

The suspended 9th is retained, or held on, or suspended, instead of the root of a chord, to which root it must proceed while the chord continues. The root may be sounded as a bass together with the 9th, but has an extremely harsh effect if taken in any of the upper parts simultaneously with the discord that is to resolve upon it.

The first inversion of a suspended 9th has the 3rd of the chord in the bass. The inverted 9th now appears as the 7th from the bass; which being resolved upon the 6th—the inverted root—we have our now familiar first inversion of a concord.

The last inversion of a suspended 9th has the 9th itself in the bass, which being resolved upon the root, we have then the common chord in its direct original position. The 3rd and 5th of the original chord stand as 2nd and 4th to the inverted 9th, and regain their normal names when the 9th is resolved.

The suspended 4th is continued instead of a 3rd of a chord, upon which 3rd it is resolved before the harmony changes.

Suspended 4th.

The first inversion of a suspended 4th has the 3rd of the original chord in the bass, which bass should be approached by the ascent of a 2nd, since this gradual approach lessens the otherwise too great harshness of the discord. In this first inversion the original 4th stands as a 9th from the bass; and the chord is distinguished from the original form of the suspended 9th, by being accompanied with the 6th instead of the 5th.

In the last inversion of the suspended 4th, the 4th itself is the bass; which being resolved upon the 3rd, we have then of course the first inversion of a concord. In this case, the 5th and root of the original chord stand at the intervals of a 2nd and 5th from the inverted 4th, and remaining, become the 3rd and 6th of the note on which this is resolved;

the rough, clear, masculine character of the suspended 4th is very conspicuous in the situations where this combination is written by the old contrapuntal masters, which are so frequent that its use is felt to be one of the most obvious distinctions of the style of these composers, and is therefore commonly practised by modern musicians when they wish to give an antique savour to any particular passage. I shall recur to this subject when, in a future lecture, explanation is made of the consonant 4th, peculiar to modern music; but as it is one of much significance in discriminating the general effect of the two broad styles of music, it merits this brief pause to impress it particularly on your attention.

The suspensions of the 9th and the 4th, and their inversions, can be held over any concord or inversion of a concord. To exemplify this, let us take as a bass the descending scale in a major key, accompanying each note with a first inversion, and suspend the root of every chord as the inverted 9th of the chord that follows it;

and again, in the same succession of concords, let us suspend every bass note as the inverted 4th of the chord that follows it;

and it is manifest that each note of the key may be suspended, either as an inverted 9th in an upper part of the harmony, or as an inverted 4th in the bass. Where, however, a common chord may be taken with its root in the bass, then may either of these suspensions be held over such root; but where a concord can only be taken in an inverted form, it is only over such inversion that the suspensions can be held.

<small>Suspended 5th</small>
It has been shown that the mediant and the leading-note cannot be employed as the bass of common chords, because of the dissonance of the 5th to each of these as a bass note. These dissonant 5ths are taken, however, as suspensions, which must resolve on the 6th of the same bass notes.

- The dissonant 5th on the leading note is the same diminished 5th whether the key be minor or major.

The dissonant 5th of the mediant of the minor key is an augmented 5th—this being the only situation where, in the diatonic style, the interval of the augmented 5th occurs; and it is claimed to be diatonic on the ground that, though marked by an accidental, the leading note is essential to the minor key as distinguishing this from the major key with the same signature, and the minor 3rd is equally essential to the minor key as distinguishing it from the major of the same tonic. There is a poignancy, a pathos, an intensity of expression in the effect of this suspension of the augmented 5th, which anticipates rather the delicate tenderness of the chromatic style than seems naturally akin to the rough terseness of the diatonic; we have seen, however, that its employment is fully compatible with diatonic principles, and its beauty renders its very sparing use, but not its abuse, one of the richest adornments of the class of music to which it has been shown generically to belong.

Analogous to the effect of the suspension last described, but not making us so yearn—may one say—for its resolution, is that of the 5th on the mediant of the major key; the dissonant character of which springs from the peculiar relationship, or, to speak better, the non-relationship of the tritone, between the subdominant in a preceding chord and the leading note in this.

---

* Though the impression may remain on some ears, of the G from the preceding chord, this note is not sounded together with the bass D, and so the interval of the 4th from the bass is not presented in the harmony.

The suspension of the dissonant 5ths, being the retardation of the roots of chords in the first inversion, belongs specially to this form of the dominant and tonic chords with their 3rd in the bass; unlike suspensions of the 9th and 4th, since these may be taken wherever the concords may be taken on which they must resolve.

Double suspension. Double suspension is the holding both the 9th and 4th together over the root and 3rd of a chord;

or the inverted 9th and dissonant 5th, which both resolve upon the root; or the inverted 4th added to this last combination, which is resolved on the inverted 3rd—being the octave of the bass note.

Their first employment is ascribed to Claudio Monteverde, who lived in the latter part of the sixteenth century and beginning of the seventeenth, and was as much castigated as applauded by critics of his era, for the invention of these and other harmonies, all of which they denominated his "new discords."

Florid forms of melody. A particular form of melody, signally characteristic of the diatonic style, arises from the leap of a sus-

pended note to some consonance, and the return—
either by leap or passing notes—to its resolution.

The use of this ornate figure is frequent in contrapuntal writing, to which it imparts emphatic point that strongly distinguishes the phrases of melody which are often repeated in imitation by the several voices.

A complete chord may be suspended when the progression of roots is by the rise of a 4th or fall of a 5th. When this is the case, the notes that are dissonant from the second root are not restricted, as the single intervals would be were these separately suspended, to a particular resolution as 9th or 7th of the bass; but, provided they move no more than a 2nd, these dissonant notes are free to rise or fall as they would were the progression without suspension from the first to the second chord.

Suspension of complete chords.

The suspension of complete chords, now described, in admissible only when the progression of roots is by a 4th or its inversion a 5th; this rule of progression appears to point by analogy to the relationship between the dominant and tonic, and foreshadows in some respect the speciality of the class of discords next to be discussed.

<small>Essential discords.</small>   Both passing-notes and suspensions, you must have noticed, are notes foreign or inessential to the harmony, either passing from, or held instead of, some note of the chord. Essential discords, on the contrary, are constituent notes of the harmony; and they are distinguished from suspensions by being resolved, together with the entire chord of which they are integral portions, upon some chord having another root. This root of the chord which constitutes the resolution of all discords of the class now under consideration, is invariably the 4th above or 5th below the root of the discord that is to be resolved upon it; and the need for such radical progression is the point of affinity, to which I just now alluded, between the essential discords and the suspension of complete chords. The essential discords are the 5th on the mediant, in both minor and major keys, and the 5th on the supertonic in a minor key; the 7th on any note, the 4th above which may be the root of a chord; and the 9th, under the same conditions as the 7th. The dissonant note, whether 5th, 7th, or 9th, must be prepared,—previously sounded, that is, as a concord; but, unlike a suspension, it has its resolution

on a note of the *following* harmony, not of the *same* chord.

The chord of the dissonant 5th of the mediant is the same combination of notes as the suspended 5th on the same degree of the scale, its distinction from which is seen in its different resolution; for, whereas the suspended 5th rises to the inverted root of the same chord, _{Essential 6th on mediant.}

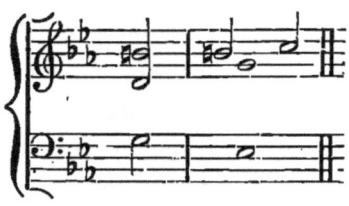

the 5th, as an essential discord, rises to the 3rd of a chord of another root.

The same harmony may be inverted with its 3rd in the bass; and then though the bass rise but a 2nd, the radical relation of the two chords is the same as when both have their roots in the bass; notice, in illustration of this, the names of the roots in letters under the discord and its resolution in the next example.

76 THE ANCIENT STRICT OR DIATONIC STYLE.

Essential 7th.   A prepared 7th may be added to the chord of the dissonant 5th, which must fall to the 3rd of the following chord.

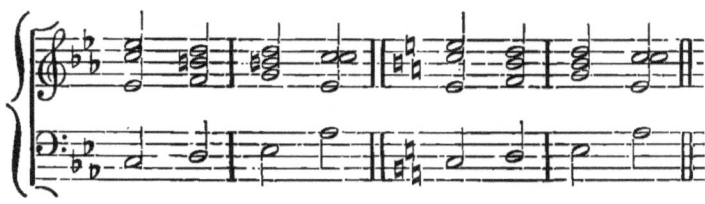

The 7th may also be sounded without the 5th, when its treatment is the same as if the 5th accompanied it.

A 7th may, in like manner, be added to a common chord; the 5th in which, being a concord, suffers no change by the addition of the 7th.

Observe the grand, ponderous effect of a succession of these chords of the 7th, each resolved upon another, constituting a sequence throughout the entire scale.

The first inversion of a chord of the 7th has its 3rd in the bass, which either rises a 2nd to the root of the next chord,

78   *THE ANCIENT STRICT OR DIATONIC STYLE.*

or is repeated as the 7th in this following harmony.

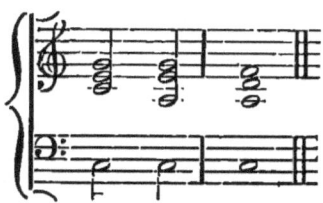

The last chord in the foregoing example is the last inversion of a chord of the 7th, where the 7th itself is the bass, which must be resolved—as duly as when it is placed in an upper part—by descent to the 3rd of the following chord.

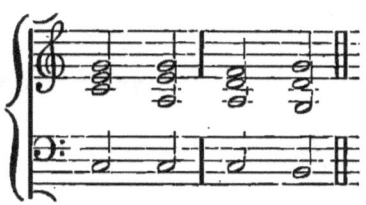

In this form, with the dissonant note in the bass, a chord of the 7th has a character of forcible imperious expression which is unparalleled by that of any other combination; and when the chord occurs at an emphatic part of a phrase, its powerful effect strikes every listener.

Essential 5th on supertonic.   The diminished 5th on the supertonic of a minor key has so unsatisfactory and ambiguous an effect when sounded by itself, that it is not available in harmony except it be accompanied with a 7th, which defines its root and its treatment; it is then resolved on the root of the next chord, which stands a 2nd below it.

A prepared 9th may be added to a chord of the 7th, as was the 9th to a triad; and this 9th must be resolved on the 5th of the succeeding chord. *Essential 9th.*

The harshness would be too great of the sound of the root together with the 9th, were the root taken in any other part than the bass; it is requisite, therefore, to omit the root in all the inversions of the chord of the 9th. The first inversion, having the 3rd of the chord for its bass, thus appears like the original direct position of a chord of the 7th;

80   THE ANCIENT STRICT OR DIATONIC STYLE.

but it is distinguished from this by its resolution, which, in the case of the inverted 9th, is on a chord whose root is the note next above the previous bass note, which is the 4th above the root of the said previous chord; whereas, in the case of the original 7th, the root of the resolution is the 4th above the bass of the discord, since this bass is then the root.

The second inversion of a chord of the 9th has the 5th in the bass, when the original 9th stands at the interval of a 5th from the bass.

In the two inversions already described of the chord of the 9th, the 7th of the original chord is consonant with every note that is sounded in the harmony. As preparation is required to lessen the asperity of a dissonance; as resolution is needed to satisfy, nay, console the ear after the effect of such harshness; and as neither preparation nor resolution is a merely ceremonious form of respect shown to a note in consideration of the name it bears; the original 7th being in those two cases no discord, needs, as the examples have shown, neither preparation nor resolution. It is not, however, thus exempt in the last available inversion of the chord, when the said 7th, being the bass, forms a dissonance against the 4th above it, which is the 3rd of the original chord; and because it is now dissonant—not because it is named 7th—it must now be prepared and resolved as indispensably as the original 9th, which is the third of the present bass note.

The term relative, as applied to a major and a minor key that have the same signature, has been carefully explained. Other keys are also called relative. They are, 1st, those which have one sharp more or one flat less than the original key—namely, the dominant and its relative minor in a major key, and the dominant and its relative major in a minor key; and 2nd, those which have one sharp less or one flat more than the original key—namely, the subdominant and its relative minor in a major key, and the subdominant and its relative major in a minor key. These

Relative keys.

keys are related to the original by reason of the many notes, and consequently many harmonies, that each has in common with the key that is central to them all. Modulation—the transition from key to key in the course of a piece of music—is made with good effect from any of these keys to either of the others; their common affinity to the central tonic being a bond of union, a principle of gravitation, that holds them all in tonal relationship to one another.

This general explanation of the harmonies peculiar to the ancient strict style, and of some figures of melody which are consequent upon their employment, let me hope, may direct your attention to the salient characteristics of music composed until nearly the middle of the seventeenth century. Admirable examples of the more complicated application of these diatonic principles exist in the ecclesiastical works and in the madrigals of the early Flemish, Roman, and English schools, which I trust you will hear with a sharper relish for knowing under what trammels the masters wrought who produced them. This much of insight, into the merits of a style now superseded, but not obsolete, will also, I flatter myself, form such an approach to an investigation of the rules of modern harmony, as will materially aid in the comprehension of its establishment upon natural instead of conventional principles, and its consequently scientific basis.

LECTURE III.

THE MODERN FREE OR CHROMATIC STYLE.

IT is now to discuss the Chromatic style of harmony; before entering upon the details of which, let us stay to examine the signification of its generic title.

Chromatic—*coloured*—would seem to be an epithet more appropriate to plastic than to tonal art, in which latter its use is indeed figurative. Such at least is the case in modern music; the Greeks, however, are said by some to have used this word, chromatic, to denote the genus that was between the diatonic and the enharmonic, the two extremes, as visual colours are between the two extremes of white and black; and they are said by others to have employed the word, still more prosaically, in reference to a coloured string of the lyre used for the inflected note in the chromatic tetrachord. With us, the term chromatic vividly suggests the obvious distinction between the grand, cold, hard simplicity—purity, if you will—of the ancient style, and the more minute, more glowing, softer ornamentation that variegates our modern music. The change which has slowly crept over the aspect of our art during the last two centuries and a half, may be likened to that which would be seen in a spacious hall, wherein the gradations of light and shade were the only relief to the whiteness of the marble of which it was constructed; and the same hall illuminated by the sunshine streaming in through richly stained windows, whose gorgeous dyes it painted on the architectural elaboration. The secularization of the musical art divested it, fold after fold, by fine and lingering degrees, of the stony frigidity of convention, and rendered it at once capable of human expression and appellant to human sympathy; the sculptured Galatea of Pygmalion received animation, the hue of life blushed upon her cheeks, the pulse of passion beat at her heart, the voice of love breathed from her lips while its electric dart flashed from her eyes, and the arbitrary formalities of art melted into the emotional freedom of nature.

Exceptional treatment of tonic, dominant, and subdominant.

The first glimmer of the modern style of music was perhaps the discovery of the peculiar tonal relationship that exists between the tonic and dominant with the concords that accompany them in every key; and the next ray of light that gleamed upon the then narrow horizon of musical theory must have been that of another relationship between every tonic and its subdominant. Here then was an infraction of the diatonic principle that applied the same unexceptional laws to the government of every note in the key; since these special relationships of the tonic to its dominant and to its subdominant exacted a particular treatment of that note with its chord in reference to each of the others.

5ths and 8ths.

The progression by similar motion to the 5th or 8th of any bass note, which had been universally forbidden,

was found to lose all its objectionable effect when the progression lay between the chord of the key-note and either of those others, with the single reservation that the upper part in such progressions approached the 5th or 8th by the step of a 2nd.

Nay, further, the progression from 5th to 5th, or from 8th to 8th—the so-called consecutive 5ths and 8ths that are the terror of all young students in harmony—was authoritatively forbidden in all precept and scrupulously avoided in all practice;

but its use, however rare, by composers of the present century, proves that this most stringently proscribed progression may produce an effect of measureless beauty, when it lies between the chord of the tonic and either of those whose exceptional relation to this we are now considering, provided only that, in case of 8ths, the parts that have the two in succession proceed by contrary motion.

SINFONIA PASTORALE.—*Beethoven.*

SONATA, Op. 53.—*Beethoven.*

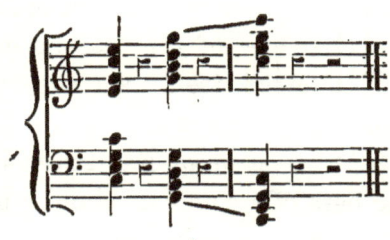

I may recur here to what has been already advanced as to the faculty of the tutored ear for adjusting the prevarications of equal temperament; the 5th of a key-note and of its dominant, or of a key-note and its subdominant, are, in the scale of nature, perfectly true in intonation as compared with each other, which is not the fact with any other two diatonic 5ths in the same key; equal temperament gives equal imperfection to all intervals in all keys, but the ear accepts for what they should be these exceptionally perfect 5ths in every key, and hears in them what nature would produce rather than what is positively sounded.

To this wondrous faculty of adjustment in the human ear must be attributed the sensation we experience, not of something negatively unobjectionable, to be tolerated, but of an effect of positive beauty, when we hear, in a passage to which their rich ample sonority is appropriate, these 5ths of the tonic and dominant or tonic and subdominant in consecution.

It belongs rather to the province of acoustics than of music to probe the reasons for the most repulsive effect produced by the prohibited progressions of 5ths or 8ths; their investigation at least would far outstep the limits of the present occasion.

Mention was made in our first lecture of the exceptionally sensitive character of the leading-note—the 7th of a key. This forced itself upon the consideration of writers in the ancient style, in the fact that this leading-note, by reason of its diminished 5th, could not be the bass of a common chord; but, partially limited as it was on this account in its combination with other notes, its progressional treatment was in no wise different from that of other notes of the key; and in the music of these composers, it rises or falls or remains as would any other note. The perception of the marked peculiarity of this note has only been fully matured within some hundred years of the present time; for although musicians of the preceding century anticipated the most extreme chromatic harmonies of our newest age, they paid no regard to the special requirements of this note, by which we distinguish it from every other. The modern cultivated ear, however, has so lively a sense

Leading-note.

of the special nature of the leading-note, that its duplication in a chord is repugnant to us,

and we desire, or rather demand, the ascent of this note in progressing from chord to chord.

More strikingly exceptional indeed, in its effect and in its treatment, is now the leading-note than any other degree of the diatonic scale; and the necessity I have stated for its rising to a note of the following chord, ceases only when it is employed as one of the prepared discords of the diatonic style, or as a passing-note.

Second inversion of concords. Next in order, appears to have been the discovery that the interval of a 4th from the bass, when this is produced by inverting the root of a chord above its 5th,

has not the dissonant effect that distinguishes it in all the combinations described at out last meeting. It was found that—though the suspended 4th, the inversion of the suspended 9th, and the inversion of the essential 7th were all discords—the root of a chord in all positions, direct or inverted, was, and is, and ever will be a concord.

The admission that the inverted 5th is a consonant 4th, gives a second inversion of concords in the modern, free style of music; but the availability of this second inversion—namely, a chord with its 5th in the bass, is peculiar to the three common chords of whose exceptional nature I have just spoken.

At first the second inversion of the tonic chord Tonic. only was used, and even this rarely, save under the circumstances that would license the employment of any other chord upon a pedal.

Freely and frequently as this chord is now written, I may yet direct your attention to two rhythmical positions wherein its effect is perhaps more notable than elsewhere; I., as the chord immediately preceding a half close, to which it often given a lingering sweetness;

MESSIAH.—*Handel.*

II., as the chord preceding that of the dominant in approaching a full close.

From the same.

Subdominant.

The second inversion of the subdominant chord came next into use; but, however the frequency has increased of the employment of its elder sister, this second inversion of the subdominant has always been and still is more seldom written than that of the chord of the key-note.

THE MODERN FREE OR CHROMATIC STYLE. 91

SONGS WITHOUT WORDS.—*Mendelssohn.*

It was scarcely until the present century that com- *Dominant.* posers adopted a second inversion of the dominant common chord, which therefore may be described as the last of the only three available second inversions of concords.

SONATA IN E, Op. 14.—*Beethoven.*

I strongly particularized, last week, the character- *Suspended* istic effect of the suspended 4th of the ancient style; *4th and inverted 5th.* it is now to compare this with the effect, no less characteristic, of the inverted 5th of the modern style, and when the two are collated you cannot but observe the breadth and freedom, yet somewhat softness, of the one, as distinguished from the pointed definiteness, with all its sterile firmness and gothic grandeur, of the other.

48 FUGUES.—*Bach.*

HARPSICHORD FUGUE.—*Handel.*

The disputes of theorists are voluminous as they are inconclusive respecting the dissonance or consonance of the 4th; but they are reconcilable, as might have been the quarrel of the two knights errant who fought because one declared a certain shield to be of silver which the other asserted to be golden, by the exposition that the 4th, like the shield, has two aspects, and that both sides of the question are true.

Consonant, however, as decidedly is the second inversion of a concord—and this is proved by the entirely free progression of the 4th it comprises, which is the assumed dissonant note of the disputants—the treatment of a chord in this form has other limitations than its restriction to three notes of the key. These are—that its bass may not be approached by leap from the inversion of any other chord;

that it must be followed by a chord whose bass note is either the same as that of the second inversion, or the note next above or below this;

and that if this bass note be the same, the second inversion must occur at a more strongly accented portion of the measure than the chord which follows it.

94 THE MODERN FREE OR CHROMATIC STYLE.

Harmonics. The phenomenon that every musical sound generates others, is the basis of the free style of harmony. This phenomenon is demonstrable on every string and every pipe of length sufficient, and consequent depth of tone, for the ear to detect the more and more delicate sound of its generated notes, or harmonics, as they are technically called, when they successively become evident to the perception. The bass strings of grand pianofortes, made before the middle of the present century, give out harmonics so distinct that the ear may discern them; all wind instruments yield their harmonics—not together, indeed, but successively—to the stronger pressure of the player's breath; and those of the class of horns and trumpets have no other notes than their harmonic sounds, and the performer has no means of varying these but by the different manner in which he may direct his breath through the pipe. Instruments of the violin class have also their harmonics, which are produced by a mechanism totally different from that for intonating the consecutive notes of a scale. Visitors to the music class-room of the University of Edinburgh, since the administration of Professor Donaldson, may have witnessed experiments in harmonics upon a string sixty-four feet in length, whose complete vibrations, and whose nodal divisions up to the eleventh or twelfth ventral sections, are obvious to the eye, as clearly as its sounds are distinct to the ear. I refer to this, because so extensive an instrument, or even the space to contain it, is not easily procurable, and because you may be satisfied to know that the calculations of philosophers have been practically verified before mixed classes of observers. A smaller string has proportionally more rapid vibrations, which induce proportionally acuter sounds, and these again yield still more delicate harmonics; but, though we set in vibration a string so short that its pulses are too fine and too rapid for observation, whose harmonics are too delicate for detection, nay, whose original sound is even too acute for definition by the most sensitive musical ear, the example I have adduced compels the inference that this string, however short, has in like manner its vibrations and its harmonics, though too minute for perception by human organs. Reverse the rule of reduction, and suppose the length of the vibrating body to be doubled again and again until it endlessly multiply that of Profesor Donaldson's sixty-four-foot string, and the same process of inference teaches us that, though its original sound be far too deep for sensuous fathoming, its vibrations and its harmonics follow the same laws that have been ocularly and orally tested. Many present must have heard, for instance, the prolongation of the final notes of a choir in some vast vaulted building, whose lofty aisles seem to embrace the sounds as anxious to retain them; and must have heard new sounds spring into being among those the singers had intoned, spiritual existences, as it were, the ethereal souls of the corporeal notes of human utterance. A cathedral, being a hollow form, is an enormous pipe; and this property, which it possesses in common with the smallest wind instruments, of giving out harmonic or generated sounds, must be the reason why early musicians as a rule made their final closes upon a major chord, though the key of their piece were minor; since the major 3rd is one of the most prominent notes of the harmonic series—so prominent indeed, in buildings of great reverberation, as to jar against the minor 3rd, if this be long sustained. We have but to extend further the inferential idea of smaller or larger vibrating media, and to follow this in thought into infinity, and we may willingly acknowledge the unmeasured concave of nature to be an immense musical instrument; when the Pythagorean doctrine of the music of the spheres will cease to seem a figurative image, a scientific myth, and will appear to ordinary comprehension but the statement of a fact whose manifest evidence is within the reach of our senses.

Fundamental chords. It would be vain, in this place, to attempt the analysis of the principle that rules these generated notes; let the mere specification of the first seven notes of the harmonic series suffice for our present purpose. Any note—say C—is a generator, and its harmonics rise in the order of its 8th, 5th, another 8th, major 3rd, an octave of the 5th, and minor 7th.

This list might be extended truly without limit; but let me for the present close it here, in order to apply thus much of it to practical illustration of a grand exception from one of the most stringent rules of the contrapuntal style. This rule is that, to lessen the asperity of a discord, every dissonant note—save only passing notes—must be prepared. We learn, however, that the minor 7th, together with the major 3rd, belongs to the series of harmonics, and is thus naturally prepared whenever its generator is sounded, or is in fact co-existent with such generator; our singing or playing this combination of notes is then but a stronger articulation of sounds that already are throbbing in the air, to render them more definite to human organs; and the artificial preparation or foresounding of a dissonant note to mitigate its harshness is superseded by the affinity of this generated discord to its cognate sounds. It is of course necessary for practical musical purposes, not only to make a selection of notes from the endless harmonic series, but to confine the use of harmonics to those belonging to certain exceptional generators, or roots, in every key; otherwise every note of every chord might be supposed to furnish its harmonic series, and each of these its harmonics in turn, all sounds would comprise all other sounds, tonality would be at an end, and Babel would reign supreme.

The notes selected from the harmonic series for

Exceptional treatment of dominant, supertonic, and tonic.

the use of the musician constitute what may be called Fundamental Chords, since these chords have a tonal foundation, which is indeed the source of every note in their various ramifications.

The notes in a key that are available as roots of fundamental discords are, first in order of chronology and first in the frequency of its use, the dominant; second in historical succession and rarer in employment, the supertonic; and most modern of all and most seldom of occurrence, the key-note itself. The discords of the dominant and supertonic and tonic, being exceptionally produced, have equally exceptional treatment. The uniformity of the diatonic principle was broken through in the exceptional government of the eldest of the three; and in our future comparison of this with the laws referring to chords derived from the other two roots, I shall have to show you that the uniform progression of each dissonant note to its resolution and the uniform progression of roots prevail no longer.

Dominant 7th.

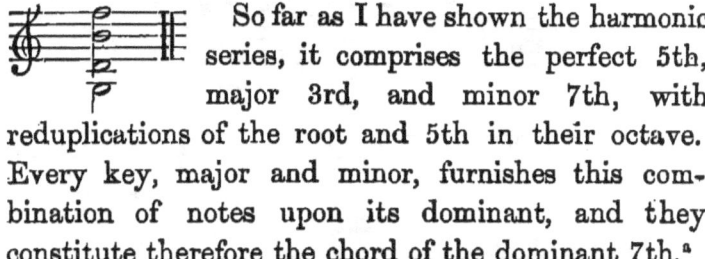

So far as I have shown the harmonic series, it comprises the perfect 5th, major 3rd, and minor 7th, with reduplications of the root and 5th in their octave. Every key, major and minor, furnishes this combination of notes upon its dominant, and they constitute therefore the chord of the dominant 7th.[a]

---

[a] It is common to ascribe the discovery and first employment of this chord to Monteverde, who has already been named as the originator of innovations that were in extension of, and not exceptional from, established rule (page 72). There are examples of the unprepared discord of the dominant seventh, however, in the music of Jean Mouton, who lived and wrote a century earlier than he.

This eminently beautiful chord of the dominant 7th, so rich, so full, so harmonious in its effect, has besides the exceptionality of needing no artificial preparation, the further and still more remarkable distinction from all the discords of the ancient style, that the ear can rest upon it with pleasure, and its resolution may, for this reason, be delayed for any indefinite time. Thus a chord of the dominant 7th may in some cases close a rhythmical period,

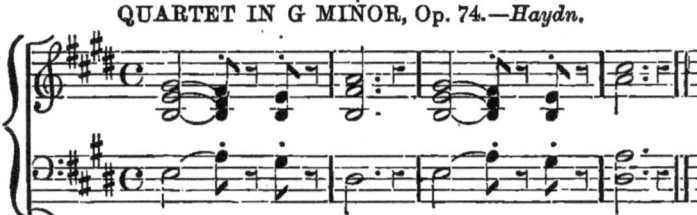

QUARTET IN G MINOR, Op. 74.—*Haydn.*

or may even have a pause upon it, which sets aside for the moment all rhythmical continuity :

SINFONIA EROICA.—*Beethoven.*

the 7th it comprises may be transferred from one to any other part in the harmony,

GRAND SUITE IN B MINOR.—*Bach.*

and this may even be employed in the same manner as the root, 3rd or 5th, for the resolution of a dissonant passing-note.

RONDO IN ♭E.—*Weber.*

Beautiful and gratifying as is its effect, it is however, for all the freedom I have just exemplified, still a discord requiring ultimate resolution; and, as if in compensation for its otherwise freedom, it has the distinction from prepared discords that its 3rd, as much as its 7th, needs to be resolved. According to the radical progression of ascending 4ths, that binds the essential discords to the chords of their resolution in the diatonic style, the chord of the dominant 7th is naturally resolved on the chord of the key-note, to the 3rd of which the 7th must fall while the leading-note rises to the root; the root and 5th of the dominant chord, forming a perfect interval with each other, have no restraint in their progression.

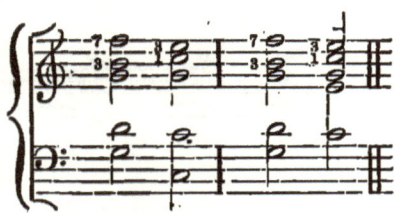

The sense will quickly learn to recognize the sound, perfectly unique in your present supposed experience, of this strongly characteristic chord; and the reason will approve this recognition by calculating the interval of the diminished 5th between the 3rd and 7th of the dominant—that interval most conspicuously individual in the strict style of music—in which this chord differs from every other chord of the 7th in the diatonic scale.

The first inversion of the chord of the dominant 7th has the leading-note in the bass; and the third inversion has the 7th in the bass; when the notes all bear the same treatment as when the chord is in its original position.

That this chord bears to be taken in the second

inversion—namely, with its 5th in the bass—further distinguishes it from prepared 7ths, in which, because of the unsatisfactory character of their inverted root as a 4th from the bass, the second inversion is unavailable.

The 5th of a chord, you will remember, when taken in the bass, is limited to proceed to the note next above or below it; this rule holds as strongly in the second inversion of a discord as of a common chord. The second inversion of the dominant 7th may then be followed by the chord of the tonic, either in its original position,

or in its first inversion.

Notice, in the last example, a further exception from the treatment of all discords hitherto explained; the 7th rises to the 5th of the tonic chord, instead of falling to its 3rd, which would be allowed to no 7th, sounded with its root, of the diatonic series; and the good effect of this progression is induced by the gradual ascent of the bass—always the most sonorous part in the harmony—to the note that would otherwise have resolved the discord. Let me remind you of a chord described at our last meeting—the anomalous first inversion, with the supertonic in the bass, of a chord comprising the diminished 5th, the inverted triad of the leading-note.* The anomaly of this inverted chord without an apparent root is now to be solved; the dominant is the root of the chord in question,

which root being omitted, the chord presents the appearance of a first inversion, in having only the 3rd and 6th of its bass note. I say the appearance; but while you admit this likeness to the eye, you must feel a striking dissimilarity between the sound of this chord and of any concord in its first inversion. This chord is, in truth, a compromise between the strict and the free styles; it contains no two notes alphabetically contiguous, nor any note at a diminished or augmented interval from the bass, nor any 4th from the bass, and consequently fulfils none of the definitions of a discord in the strict style; but it possesses the decisive, determining, commanding character of the dominant harmony from which it is derived, or, if you will, selected, and hence its availability as the chord before the tonic in a perfect cadence. The ancient inadmission of the inverted 5th

---

* Page 52.

as a consonant 4th precluded the use of the second inversion of the chord of the dominant 7th in its complete form; it is notable therefore that the root is omitted in music of so late as even the time of Handel, and its employment by later composers may be regarded as a feature of the modern style.

MESSIAH.—*Handel.*

Saith your God,   Saith your God.

FIGARO.—*Mozart.*

Oh del paggio, quel che detto,   e - ra so - lo.

Let me remind you that, in the diatonic style, the firsa inversion of a chord of the essential 9th consists of the same notes as the original position of a chord of the 7th,* but differs from this in being resolved on a chord whose root is the 2nd above its bass note. An unprepared chord of the dominant 7th is subject to

---

* Page 79.

this same treatment as the first inversion of a 9th, whose unexpressed root is supposed to be a 3rd below its sounded bass note. This treatment of the dominant 7th induces a form of interrupted cadence with which most persons who listen to music are familiar.

DON GIOVANNI.—*Mozart.*

E non ho be-ne s'el-la non ha.

It is now time to analyse the chromatic scale, and to show you therein the materials in which the music of our days is wrought—the alphabet, so to speak, of the modern style. We have seen that the diatonic scale in all major or minor keys consists of a gradual succession of notes, whose inter-relationship results from their common reference to the key-note.* The reference of each note in the diatonic scale to its key-note, is not more distinctly definite than is that of every note in the chromatic scale; convenience of writing, however, constantly tempts musicians to employ false notation in chromatic passages; and that the eye is much accustomed to the look of such expedient notation is the strongest reason for examining the true relation of all chromatic notes to their key-note, in order that we may understand the chords composed of them.

Chromatic scale.

---

* Page 24.

THE MODERN FREE OR CHROMATIC STYLE.

The chromatic scale comprises twelve notes. These are the same when reckoned from the same tonic, whether the key be minor or major; but there need, of course, different accidentals for their signification, according to whether they occur in a minor or a major key. They are I., the seven notes of the major diatonic scale, together with the three indicated by the altered signature of the minor key—namely, the minor 3rd, 6th, and 7th,—so that thus far the chromatic scale is either the diatonic major or minor scale with the addition of the notes peculiar to the other;

II., and besides these ten, to complete the number twelve, the minor 2nd intervenes between the tonic and supertonic, and the augmented 4th between the subdominant and dominant;* these last two being chromatic notes, or notes that are only expressible by accidentals, in both minor and major keys.

Chromatic concords.

I have now to prove the true application of the term chromatic, in its modern technical sense, to

---

* Pages 109 and 111.

chords, as signifying that they comprise accidentals which do not change the key. In illustration of the influence of the dominant harmony upon its key—of the domination, in fact, of the dominant—there was occasion to show you how a chord might belong to several different keys, and how the ear depended on the harmonious context for satisfaction as to whether such chord were the tonic of one key, the subdominant of another, or the dominant of yet another.[a] Every chord should belong either to the key of the passage that precedes it, as does the chord of D major to the key of G in the following example;

or to the key of the passage that succeeds it, as does also the chord of D major in the following, though the preceding passage is in the key of C.

In the first example, a modulation occurs immediately after the chord of D, which has no retrospective effect on what precedes it; in the second example, the chord of D changes the key, and thus affects the tonal character of what follows. Let me now quote a passage

---

[a] Page 27.

wherein what precedes and what succeeds the first chord marked with an accidental are both in the key of ♭B;

understanding that the chord must belong either to the key of the antecedent or to that of the subsequent harmony, and perceiving that both these are in the same key, you must acknowledge that this chord of C major induces no modulation, and must therefore be a chromatic chord in the unchanged key of ♭B. The second quotation presents the same passage in the key of G minor, as it occurs later in the movement; and here, the chord of A major has the same chromatic relation to the key of G, that, in the former case, the chord of C has to the key of ♭B.

I have now to show you what chromatic concords are thus available.

Minor 2nd. A chromatic major common chord of which the

minor 2nd of the key is the root, is employed with admirable effect in both minor and major keys;

and the first inversion of this is of more frequent occurrence.

ALEXANDER'S FEAST.—*Handel.*

SYMPHONY IN A.—*Beethoven.*

Far less frequent, but no less beautiful, is the use of the second inversion of the chromatic common chord of the minor 2nd of the key; examples might be adduced from Mozart and subsequent writers, but one may be quoted from the overture to Handel's Semele, as showing its earlier and highly effective employment.

I have traced the use of this chord so far back as the Elizabethan era; but that you may be the oftener reminded of its technical speciality by its remarkable effect, I choose rather for illustration examples of its employment from composers who have lived nearer to our own days. Let us for a moment turn back from the technical to the etymological purport of the word chromatic; let us again consider its figurative application in this latter, its primitive signification, to modern music; let us compare oral impressions with those of the visual sense, and we all must feel how vividly the blank, broad, marble, majestic simplicity of the elder music, is coloured by the introduction of this very distinctive chord, and we may at the same time readily suppose how the emotions must have been stirred, in so far as they were accessible by music, of the auditors who first witnessed its effect.

Another chromatic major common chord, and its first inversion, of which the supertonic is the root, are also employed both in major and minor keys. Though countless specimens might be cited of the admirably effective employment of this chromatic concord of the supertonic, I will, rather than detain you now, refer you to the two already quoted from Mozart's Symphony in G minor.[a] The chromatic major 3rd of this chord has the same sensitive, delicate, nervous character as the leading-note; even more exactingly than which, it requires particular treatment in its progression to a note of another chord;

Supertonic.

---

[a] Page 108.

and this is, that it must either rise a 2nd, or fall a chromatic semitone to a note of its own alphabetical name. The chromatic harmony of the supertonic further so strongly resembles a dominant chord, that, to prove its incident in the original key, and to disprove its inducing any modulation into the key of the dominant, it is requisite that the chord which follows it be one especially characteristic of the original key.

All possible analogy teaches that, having F and ♭A in the key of C, ♯C can have no harmonious congruity with these, and ♭D therefore must be the name of the note above which these stand in consonant relationship.

Again, having D and A in the key of C, ♭G cannot be accountably combined with them, and ♯F therefore must be the name of the note that forms the major 3rd with this root and 5th.

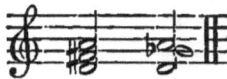

The first of these two chromatic chords shows, by its

root, that the note between the tonic and supertonic in the chromatic scale is the minor 2nd, ♭D, not an alteration of the key-note, ♯C; the second chord shows by its 3rd, that the note between the subdominant and the dominant is the augmented 4th, ♯F, not an alteration of the dominant, ♭G. The entire chromatic scale, according to the notation that has been stated, is now verified in its relation to the key-note; and its clear comprehension is the surest clue to the understanding of the chords whence it is derived, and which, as already said, are composed of it.[*]

The minor chord of the subdominant, in all its positions and inversions, is employed as a chromatic chord in the major key, especially in the modern use of the plagal cadence.

Minor subdominant.

MIDSUMMER'S NIGHT DREAM.—*Mendelssohn.*

DON GIOVANNI.—*Mozart.*

il pa-dre mio dov' è

[*] Page 106.

114   *THE MODERN FREE OR CHROMATIC STYLE.*

SONATA IN ♭E, Op. 31.—*Beethoven.*

[musical notation]

Inversion, on subdominant, of diminished triad.

Let me revert to the diatonic concords of the minor key discussed at our second meeting, and remind you of the first inversion, with the subdominant for its bass, of the diminished triad of the supertonic.[a] This also is employed as a chromatic chord in the major key.

LURLINE.—*Wallace.*

[musical notation: "To thy fate — — this heart, this heart, — — would cling."]

Minor 6th.

The major common chord of the minor 6th of the key, and its first inversion, complete the list of chro-

---
[a] Page 54.

matic concords peculiar to the major key. This chord in its original form, in alternation with the chord of the tonic, has been so often written by French composers that its use has come to be regarded as a musical Gallicism, which, quite as much as an idiomatic turn of speech, gives a national tinge to a phrase.

LES HUGUENOTS.—*Meyerbeer.*

In its inverted form, there can exist no instance more striking of its effect than the phrase in the trio in Rossini's *Guillaume Tell*, where the two conspirators, endeavouring to persuade Arnold to join their enterprise, have told him that his father's eyes have been put out by order of the tyrant; and the accompanying harmony gives all the intensity to his ejaculation of heartrending agony.

116   *THE MODERN FREE OR CHROMATIC STYLE.*

It is of future consequence here to observe that all the diatonic concords of a minor key, except only the common chord of the key-note, are employed as chromatic chords in the major key of the same tonic; but the chords peculiar to the major key are not similarly available in the minor. Hence you will perceive that the major key practically includes the minor; and I believe that, were this the time for their discussion, ample theoretical grounds for the fact might be adduced.

Free passing notes. An important exceptionality and an obvious characteristic of the free style, is the modern treatment of passing notes. Its exceptionality consists, I., in their comprising chromatic notes, which must always be quitted semitonically, save when, as was explained and exemplified when I spoke of the diatonic style, they leap to the note beyond their resolution and are resolved on the intermediate note;[a]

OVERTURE TO EURYANTHE.—*Weber.*

[a] Page 64.

II., that they may be approached, indifferently, by degrees, as in the diatonic style, or by leap;

SONATA, Op. 14.—*Beethoven.*

and III., that they may occur, also indifferently, on the unaccented divisions of a bar as in the diatonic style, or on those strongly accented.

In this last case, they are named *Appoggiaturas*, Appoggiatura. from the word Appoggiare, to lean, as signifying that they are to bear particular stress, to take all force from the following note, and to be made as conspicuous by their manner of performance as they are in their harmonic relationship. The use of these accented passing-notes is scarcely a hundred years old; and it may probably be traced to a practice of solo performers, more common with vocalists than instrumentalists, of enhancing the expression of a phrase by introducing a note above or below its most emphatic note. Composers adopted this executants' embellishment, and incorporated the written Appoggiatura in their music. For many years, however, we may suppose them to have been ashamed of the look of a note foreign to the harmony upon the strong accent of the bar; for they equivocated between its good effect and its unlawful aspect, by writing the Appoggiatura in a small character, but understanding that it was to be sung with great pressure of power, and to take half the time from the note before which it was written.

SONATA.—*Mozart.*

Another class of note, the *Acciaccatura*—a note to be crushed into the following note, or played all but together with it—was also written in a small character, and the ambiguous notation of the Appoggiatura left great uncertainty as to whether the small sign indicated a leaning note or a crushing note. This diffident but doubtful method of writing the Appoggiatura, so as to insinuate rather than define its manner of performance, remained in vogue to some extent even within these fifty years; an unfortunate result of which is, that executants of the present day sometimes mistake the appoggiatura for the acciaccatura, and substitute the brisk, quaint, brilliant effect of the one for the tender, languishing expression of the other. A nice discrimination of the character of the passage wherein such a note occurs, and of the musical meaning to be conveyed in it, is the best guide for a performer of true feeling to escape from perverting a composer's purport where he has been thus modestly indefinite in its signification. Musicians have grown bolder in our times of revolution and reform, and they are no longer afraid to write what they mean; in defiance of appearances, their Appoggiatura stands, with unblushing distinctness, in as full-sized a character as the harmony note on which it is resolved, so that, in the music of now-a-days, there is in such cases less discretion left to the performer, and as to the length of the notes, at least, far less responsibility.

SONATA, Op. 22.—*Beethoven.*

You may notice great discrepancy between the ordinary notation of chromatic passing-notes and the chromatic scale as I have explained it. You must remember, however, that I alluded to the prevalent custom of deviating occasionally from the true nomenclature of chromatic notes, upon grounds of expediency. This custom applies greatly to passing notes, and the expediency that prompts it is to economize the trouble of the reader, and perhaps also of the writer, by reducing the number of accidentals. If, for instance, the note between D and E be named ♭E, there will need an accidental natural to contradict the flat that indicates it; but, if this note be named ♯D, there will need no second accidental for the following E. Whatever licence be current in this respect, composers of every school—we must distinguish these from persons who write music of no school whatever—never miscall the augmented 4th of the key, incorrectly writing it a diminished 5th,

not

even though it cost an accidental the more for its contradiction. The reason of this is, that, in the key of C for example, ♭G would suggest so extraneous a tonality, that most players might pause to consider the propriety of any harmony, peculiar to the key of C, which might accompany or follow it.

The knowledge is, however, by no means futile of the true notation of the chromatic scale, notwithstanding the frequent derelictions from its use ; since, to know the name of a note is to know its relationship to other notes, and hence, to know the rules for its treatment. This will become more and more evident from an insight into the derivation and resolution of chromatic fundamental discords, into whose examination I shall have the pleasure to enter at our next meeting

LECTURE IV.

THE MODERN STYLE—*continued*.

IN continuing the examination of the modern or chromatic style of harmony, I must repeatedly remind you of the natural origin of Fundamental Chords—the chords I mean, that are composed of the harmonic notes generated, according to the eternal laws of sound, by the fundamental roots which are available in each key. I have offered you a technical analysis of a combination of notes that must be familiar in the daily experience of every person conversant with music, forming the eminently rich chord known as the dominant 7th; and I have now to show that this natural harmony may be imitated, by means of chromatic modifications of the diatonic scale, upon the supertonic and also upon the tonic without involving any change of tonality. As no single chord can determine a key, and as every chord belongs to the key either of the foregoing or of the following passage, if what goes before and what comes after any particular chord be both in the same key, this chord induces no modulation, but, should it comprise accidentals, is a chromatic chord in the key that is common to the preceding and succeeding passages. You have had ample proof of the integrity to their key of the several chromatic concords; you will now perceive that chromatic discords derived from the roots I have named, however they colour the effect, disturb not the certainty of the prevailing tonic.

The chromatic common chord of the supertonic— *Chromatic supertonic 7th.* which comprises the augmented 4th of the key, and which gives this note to the chromatic scale—is identical in its intervals with the common chord of the dominant, which chord it much resembles in its treatment, so far at least as regards its chromatic major 3rd, whose exigencies are as stringent as those of the leading-note. The addition of a 7th to this chord forms the same combination of intervals that composes the chord of the dominant 7th, the root and perfect 5th being free in their progression, the major 3rd and minor 7th needing to be resolved.

To identify this chord with its key, to show that it is a chromatic supertonic harmony effecting no modulation, and not the dominant harmony of another key, it must be followed by some chord peculiar to, or characteristic of, the original and permanent tonic. Two resolutions of this chord are so much more frequent than others, that they may be particularized as the characteristic or natural resolutions of the supertonic discord; and these let us separately examine.

One of these natural resolutions is when the chromatic chord of the supertonic 7th proceeds to a dominant discord. Were the chord with which the last example ended followed by a common chord of G, our impression would be, in most cases, that the passage closed in the key of G, and that ♯F was the leading-note which proceeded to G, its tonic.

If, instead of this progression, ♯F were to fall chromatically to ♮F the 7th of G, the chord of the resolution would then be the dominant, and that which preceded it, consequently, the chromatic supertonic chord in the key of C.

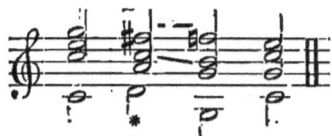

The difference between the dominant and supertonic discords is, that the former may be followed by the final note of a phrase ; whereas, the supertonic, being followed by an inconclusive harmony, more commonly occurs as at least the third chord from the end, so leading us earlier to expect the cadence, which it thus may be said to extend backwards, towards the beginning of the phrase.

IL TROVATORE.—*Verdi.*

sperda il sole d'un tuo sguardo la tempesta del mio cor.

The other natural resolution of the supertonic discord, is when it proceeds to an inversion of the chord of the tonic. Here there is exception from the diatonic rule that the root of the chord which resolves a discord must be a 4th above the root of such discord;[*] for, whatever the progression of the bass, the root of the tonic harmony is a 7th above that of the supertonic. There is exception also from the rule for the treatment of the 7th, which, instead of falling to the note below, remains to be a note of the next chord.

When speaking of other discords, it would have been redundant to affirm that the dissonant note might not be doubled; since, to say nothing of the access of harshness this would bring, the necessity for resolving the dissonant note, and the disallowance of the consecutive octaves or unisons that would arise were a doubled dissonance doubly resolved, amply provide against the doubling of discords. When,

---

[*] Page 74.

however, the 7th remains, its duplication induces not consecution of octaves, but repetition of one octave, which is frequent in succession of concords, and equally accordant with good effect in the resolution of a discord.

Such is the special effect of this discord, and such the peculiar relation of its dissonant note to the rest of the harmony, and to the general tonality, that the harshness which would result from the duplication of other discords is not felt in the doubling of this.

It may be regarded as a peculiar licence, that when the 7th is thus doubled while one of the notes is repeated in the following chord, the other may leap as a concord ;

and an extension of this licence permits that, though the 7th be not doubled, if the unrestricted 5th proceed to that note in the second chord which was the 7th in the first chord and so supply its resolution, the 7th is also then free to move as a concord.

It is worthy of careful note and of high admiration that, though at the beginning of the eighteenth century the strict contrapuntal laws had no authorized exceptions, and every departure from their observance was regarded as an aberration of genius, and accepted only out of reverence for the otherwise manifested musicianship of him who made it, the greatest composers of that age, Handel and Bach, and even their predecessor Purcell, anticipated the latest discoveries of modern times, and wrote those chords and those resolutions of chords whose use is commonly considered as the greatest freedom in the music of our own day. What is still more remarkable, is that Bach, at least, shows in his employment of these exceptional resources such evident regard for a ruling principle, that it would be groundless as arrogant to assume that he employed them experimentally. They appear indeed but rarely in his works as compared with the music of modern composers; but they reveal, nay, they prove, his complete insight into the system it is my present task to explain; and our admiration for the far-seeing penetration of his, and those other master-minds that could probe the harmonic mysteries which have taken many generations to unfold, must be equalled by our wonder at the prejudiced dulness of the successive theorists who remained purblind to truths which had been so brilliantly exemplified. The resolution of the supertonic 7th upon the chord of the tonic, for instance, has never been employed with more spontaneous and more charming effect, the melting away of its dissonant note into the consonance of the following chord nowhere can produce more surprising yet satisfactory gratification, the pertinacious beauty of this April note that frowns and smiles changefully as a discord and a concord is in no modern passage more felicitously introduced, than in one I shall quote from the Christmas Oratorio of Sebastian Bach, to which it is difficult to avoid adding other specimens alike old and alike interesting.

Chromatic tonic 7th.

The chord of the dominant 7th may likewise be imitated upon the tonic by the addition of a chromatic minor 7th to the common chord of this note; when, should the key be minor, the third also must be chromatic, because the major 3rd of the generator is a characteristic interval of every fundamental chord, which, though sometimes dispensed with, can never be ignored. The interval of the diminished 5th which stands naturally between the 3rd and 7th of the dominant—the leading-note and subdominant—namely, is imitated by the chromatic raising of the 3rd in the supertonic chord; and by the lowering of the 7th if the key be major, or raising of the 3rd if the key be minor, in the tonic chord. The two notes that constitute this interval of the diminished 5th, require resolution in the tonic harmony as much as in the supertonic and the dominant; while the root and perfect 5th are here, as in the analogous chords, free.

What may be regarded as the natural resolution of the chromatic chord of the tonic 7th, is when this proceeds to a dominant discord. Were the chord with which the last examples ended followed by a common chord of F, our impression would be that the passage closed in the key of F, of which the chord of C was the dominant.

The suspicion of modulating into the key of the subdominant is, however, totally refuted by the resolution of the chord of the 7th of C upon the dominant harmony; when again exceptionally from the diatonic rule, the succession of roots is by the descent instead of ascent of a 4th; and when, further, the 7th rises chromatically, instead of falling diatonically, to the 3rd of the next chord.

Perhaps because it is more seldom written, this tonic discord, with the resolution just shown, is more startling in its effect than any of the chords I have yet described; and in its unexpectedness, possibly, lies a chief part of its unquestionable beauty. Like a supertonic discord, the tonic 7th can scarcely be the penultimate chord of a phrase; and by its progression to another discord, this, like the supertonic, rather stimulates than fulfils our expectancy. The very individual effect of this resolution of the chromatic chord of the tonic 7th could not be better exemplified than in a prominent passage in Beethoven's Violin Quartet in C, where the body of sound seems to expand in resonance until the climax reaches the extreme of power and brilliancy at the entry of the dominant chord, which most definitely marks the key while its vibrations seem to beat with sanguine eagerness till it too is resolved.

The exceptional resolution of a fundamental chord of a 7th upon another whose root is a 4th *below* its own, sometimes occurs also in a progression from the dominant to the supertonic. For illustration of the charming effect of this, let me refer you to a passage in Professor Sterndale Bennett's[a] pianoforte Concerto in C minor;

here you will notice that the supertonic chord, which is exceptionally approached, follows what I have called its natural form of resolution in returning to the dominant discord, to be again approached exceptionally as before; the pretty dalliance between these two chords keeps the hearer in a vague sweetness of suspense, which gives ever-growing interest to the close of the passage.

You have observed that, when the supertonic harmony is followed by that of the dominant—the root then *rising* a 4th—the chromatic 3rd of the former chord falls a semitone to the 7th of the latter; and that, when the tonic harmony is followed by that of the dominant—the root then *falling* a 4th—the chromatic 7th of the former chord rises a semitone to the 3rd of the latter.

Parallel between supertonic and tonic chromatic discords.

---

[a] Afterwards Sir William Sterndale Bennett, M.A., D.C.L., Mus. Doc. Cantab., Professor of Music in the University of Cambridge and Principal of the Royal Academy of Music.

There is a kind of symmetry which is remarkable in this exceptional resolution of the chromatic notes in the progression of these two chords to that of the dominant, which stands as a centre between them. The symmetry, or reverse likeness of treatment, ceases not here; the 7th of the supertonic falls to the 3rd of the dominant, and the 3rd of the tonic rises to the 7th of the dominant. All the progressions in the resolution of the supertonic chord upon the dominant are, you perceive, reversed in the resolution of the tonic chord upon its dominant, just as the lines in a landscape are reversed in its reflection on the surface of the lake; the root falls instead of rising a 4th, the 3rd rises instead of the 7th falling to the next note, and the chromatic 7th rises instead of the chromatic 3rd falling a semitone. The reverse, reflected, symmetrical treatment of the supertonic and tonic discords continues yet further; if the 5th of the supertonic rise to the 3rd of the dominant—the note to which the 7th ordinarily proceeds—then the 7th with good effect also rises to the 5th in the dominant chord;

SYMPHONY IN F.—*Beethoven.*

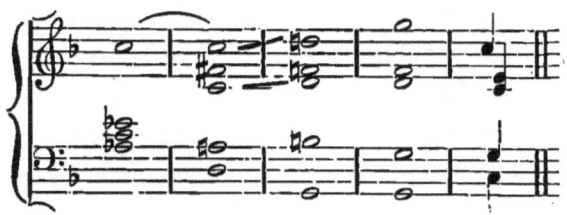

and you will trace the reflection, if the 5th of the tonic fall to the 7th of the dominant—the note to which the 3rd ordinarily proceeds—then the 3rd with equally good effect also falls to the 5th in the dominant chord.

SYMPHONY IN A MINOR.—*Mendelssohn.*

The large assemblage of numerals with which I have had to trouble you, may have given to what I have just said rather the sound of a mathematical than of a musical demonstration; most fortunate has it been if, with the sound, it have had any of the clearness of a mathematical problem, for then it will have shown you a series of facts so beautiful, and of harmonious coincidences so remarkable that there will need no further apology for applying the terms of arithmetic in explaining the materials in which genius embodies its inspirations.

The next note after the 7th in the harmonic series Dominant minor 9th.

that we have to consider is the minor 9th.[a] The addition of this note to the chord of the dominant 7th, forms the chord of the dominant minor 9th.

The four notes comprised in the chord of the 7th are unaffected, in their character or in their treatment, by the presence of this new element in the harmony; except only that the root, save under peculiar circumstances and for peculiar effects, is not sounded in any other part than the bass, because of the extreme dissonance this forms against the 9th when it appears in any of the upper parts of the harmony. There remains for me, then, but to speak of the 9th in describing the resolution of this chord.

Unlike the other four notes of the harmony, the 9th is often resolved on a note derived from its own root while the rest of the chord remains.

It is also often resolved, like the other four notes, on a note belonging to another root when the entire chord changes.

---

[a] To speak exactly, this is the 17th harmonic, but it is more conveniently described as the 8th below that note.

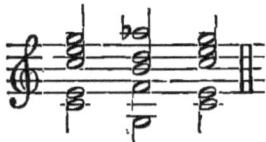

The 9th, in these two forms of its resolution, respectively resembles, to a certain extent, the suspensions and the essential discords of the diatonic style. Suspensions, you will remember, are particularly distinguished among diatonic discords by their being resolved during the continuance of the chord over which they are suspended. Discords essential to the harmony, on the contrary, are characterized by their being resolved with the change of the entire chord.

The 9th, resolved on a note derived from its own root, differs, however, from a suspension: I., in not needing to be suspended, held on, retained from the previous chord, since it may be approached wholly without preparation; II., in having a variable resolution, since it may proceed to the root or to the 3rd of the chord. When the 9th is resolved upon its root, we particularly feel it to be a note added to the chord of the 7th, the force of which it intensifies.

<small>Resolved on a note of the same chord.</small>

SONATA, Op. 29 (or 31).—*Beethoven.*

When it is resolved upon the 3rd, we feel it to be a substitution for this note, which should not therefore, then, be sounded together with the 9th, but heard only as its resolution ; the following quotation shows what tender earnestness is expressible by the resolution now described.

CONCERTO IN C MINOR.—*Beethoven.*

Resolved on a note of another chord. The natural resolution of the chord of the dominant minor 9th, when this is upon a harmony derived from another root, is the same as that of the chord of the dominant 7th—namely, upon the chord of the tonic. In this case, like the prepared essential 9th of the diatonic style, the newly added dissonance falls to the 5th of the following chord.

SONATA IN C MINOR.—*Mozart.*

As I have said, the root, except as a bass note, is rarely sounded together with the 9th; in its several inversions, therefore, the chord of the minor 9th is generally incomplete, by reason of the omission of its root. Such incompleteness is not peculiar to the chord of the 9th. The second inversion of the chord of the dominant 7th, let me remind you, is now frequently, and in elder times was regularly, written without the root; and though, from its containing no discord of technical definition, this aspect of the dominant harmony was regarded formerly as a concord, I think you must be convinced of its true derivation from the dominant, and of its being the veritable, though incomplete, chord of the dominant 7th.[*] Again, it is not at all rare for the 5th to be omitted from any chord;

---

[*] Page 103.

and even the root is sometimes absent from a combination of notes that can be accounted for in no way but as the first inversion of a common chord.

General dictionaries may teach that the word inversion signifies turning a thing—a chord for example—upside down; or, in respect to the notes of a chord, placing them all in a different relationship, as regards higher and lower, to each other. Practically, an inverted chord does not necessarily comprise every integral note of the harmony; and if the term inversion be unjust as an exact definition, it is satisfactory, because it is commonly understood; and it must be sufficient, because matters would be worse perplexed were another term to be coined.

With its 3rd in the bass, the chord of the minor 9th appears, as does the first inversion of a prepared chord of the 9th, like a chord of the 7th in its original position; and the second, third, and fourth inversions of the chord of the 9th appear like the first, second, and third inversions of a chord of the 7th.

I say appear, but such appearance belongs to the written characters only; the combination of sounds they represent is so individual, that every musical ear can trace them to the source of their natural derivation. Many musical grammarians, however, name these incomplete forms of the chord from the notes they comprise, regardless of the generator from which they are all derived. By these writers, the first inversion of the chord of the minor 9th is named the chord of the diminished 7th, the interval from the bass note to the utmost discord being that of a diminished 7th; and they describe the higher inversions of the 9th, according to their appearance, as inversions of the so-called chord of the diminished 7th. This chord depends not, as do the incomplete inversions of chords of the prepared 9th, upon the chord of its resolution to indicate its root; the internal constitution of the chord of the minor 9th, the peculiar intervals of which it is composed, prove its fundamental, harmonic, or generative derivation, and unmistakably individualize its effect. An infallible quest for the true root of this chord, in whatever inversion it may be written, may be made in the descent by 3rds, from interval to interval—avoiding the inflection by flat or sharp of any note whose natural form is sounded in the chord and avoiding the enharmonic diesis or twofold name of one pianoforte key—until the note be reached that has a perfect 5th and major 3rd among the notes of the chord.

Supertonic minor 9th.

The dominant chord of the minor 9th is imitated on the supertonic by the addition of a minor 9th to the chromatic chord of the 7th derived from this root.

The 9th in this chord, like that in the chord of the dominant, may be resolved on the root or on the 3rd while the rest of the chord remains; but it is more frequently resolved with the change of the entire chord. In this latter case, the chord of the supertonic minor 9th mostly appears in one of its inversions, when, for reasons already set forth, the root is mostly omitted.

Following, in what may still be best accounted its natural resolution, the same course as the supertonic harmony without a 9th, this chord is often resolved on a dominant discord. If the dominant discord be then resolved on a tonic discord, and that in turn upon a supertonic discord, a succession of inverted 9ths or diminished 7ths may be carried through the entire chromatic scale, the whole of whose twelve notes are comprised in the three chords that are thrice repeated in different inversions in the following examples, where the initial letters indicate which is supertonic, dominant, and tonic, and the figures show which interval of each chord is the bass note.

With equal propriety this succession of chords may be reversed, when tonic proceeds to dominant, this to supertonic, and this to tonic again.

It would not be desirable to prolong such a passage to the extent of the above examples; one section or more of either of these frequently occurs with excellent effect, and the good taste and nice feeling of a composer are well shown in the discrimination of the boundary of beauty, since this must necessarily vary with the ideas of which such a course of harmony is the expression. Some ingenious authors amusingly explain all musical effects as imitations of the natural noises we may daily witness, such as the chirping of birds, the rippling of water, the howling of tempests, and the like; and, however unacceptable, however untenable the proposition as a whole, we must all admit that it derives some odour of verity from a comparison of the chromatic progressions I have just shown you, with the sound of wind roaring through crevices, when our fear, or our solitude at least, quickens our perception.

The other natural resolution of the supertonic minor 9th (or diminished 7th on the augmented 4th of the key), is when it proceeds to the harmony of the keynote. Of its progression to a tonic discord, you have seen instances in the third and first chords of each bar in the last example of the ascending chromatic scale. In its progression to a tonic concord, if this be minor, the 9th remains to be the 3rd of the following chord, the stern, rugged effect of which may be judged from the following extract.

SONATA IN A MINOR.—*Mozart.*

If the tonic chord be major, the minor 9th of the supertonic rises chromatically to the third of the following chord.

SONATA, Op. 29 (or 31).—*Beethoven.*

* Radically ♭G, as in the first bar, not ♯F.

THE MODERN STYLE. 143

SYMPHONY, THE POWER OF SOUND.—*Spohr.*

QUARTET IN D.—*Beethoven.*

In this case, especially in the higher inversions, it is very common to write the 9th as a sharp of the note below, in order to save an accidental for its contradiction. The bright effect of this resolution supersedes all commentary, and would render futile any expletives that could be brought to bear upon its description.

The chord of the dominant minor 9th is also imitated with chromatic notes upon the tonic. Its use is exemplified in the two forms I have shown you of the harmonization of the chromatic scale. The appearance of this chord of the minor 9th is often disguised by false notation, but if the succeeding chord have a supertonic root (as in the above descending chromatic

Tonic minor 9th.

---

^a Radically ♮C, not ♯B.   ^b Radically ♮F, not ♯E.

144 THE MODERN STYLE.

scale), or a dominant root (as in the above ascending scale), the discerning ear may always identify the harmony in question with the key-note as its generator.

False notation. It is here to dilate somewhat on this matter of false notation. When speaking of chromatic passing-notes, I had occasion to admit the expediency, or at least acknowledge its frequent adoption, of misnaming chromatic notes, in order to avoid the practical inconvenience of reading or writing a second accidental which would contradict the first.[a] The same practice is, less generally, but yet not rarely, applied to the notation of chromatic chords. A half-sighted utilitarian might interpose that notation was a matter of indifference, because, through the prevalent system of equal temperament, the several notes represented by one pianoforte key—as C, ♯B, ♭♭D—have, upon every keyed instrument, all the same sound. The lens of such an observer includes but half the object, however, and the utility of his contracted observation stops short just where it is wanted to be useful. The proposition invites two answers; you shall hear them both.

I. I have offered you more than one proof that, in despite of equal temperament, the ear has the admirable faculty of so adjusting the tempered sounds which enter it, that they seem to us not what we hear, but what we should hear were all the notes perfectly attuned to the true natural scale. Thus, the sound produced by the very same pianoforte key makes a

---

- Page 120.

different impression upon us when it is employed as the 3rd of one chord, and when as the 5th of another. Let us, for example, in the key of E minor, take the chord of the dominant 7th; let us treat this according to the diatonic rule whose application to the dominant harmony I last week illustrated, regard this as the first inversion of a chord of the 9th; and so resolve it upon the chord of the submediant;[a] and, again according to the diatonic rule, let us suspend the complete chord over the bass of its resolution;[b] the notation of the suspended chord will then be C, A, #D, #F, and the #F will naturally fall to the 3rd of C, whether we construe the said #F as the 5th of B or as the 7th of the implied G root.

This must be opposed by another example; let us in the key of C take the chord of the supertonic minor 9th with its 7th in the bass, and resolve this upon the common chord of the key-note; the notation will then be C, A, ♭E, #F, and the ear will most imperiously demand that the #F rise to the 5th of C, since here the #F can only be interpreted as the chromatic 3rd of D.

---

[a] Page 104.   [b] Page 73.

I appeal to the sensuous impressions you have received from these two passages, for corroboration of what I have affirmed—namely, that ♯F, the diatonic 5th of the dominant in the key of E, has a positively different sound from ♯F, the chromatic 3rd of the supertonic in the key of C; and that thus, however it be named on paper, the true ♭E in the latter example, is a distinctly different note and produces a different effect from the ♯D in the former. To place this beyond question needs only to reverse the progression of the F in the two cases, making that accompanied with ♯D rise to G, and that accompanied with ♭E fall to E, and the bad effect of both will carry conviction on its front.

II. Granting, however, that the business of the reader is to strike the keys indicated by the written notes, regardless of antecedence, consequence, and relationship; the etymology of a chord is all-important to the composer, since the progression of every note in a fundamental discord depends upon its relationship to the root; and this relationship can only be shown by the notation. The writer, then, must know the orthography of a chord if he will have certainty as to its treatment; knowing this, if he choose to take off his college cap in deference to expediency, the matter rests between him and his conscience, which is sometimes personified by his publisher, and no one suffers seriously but the analytical critic from his device.

Some of the most exquisite effects in music are produced by enharmonic changes of one or more notes in a chord, so as to alter its root, and the key consequently to which it belongs. The four notes in the first inversion of a chord of the minor 9th, standing at the interval of a minor 3rd above each other, may either or all of them change their names for any other that are represented by the same pianoforte key. In my two last examples, the alteration of ♯D, into ♭E changes the root of the chord from B to D, and the key to which it belongs is changed accordingly. *[margin: Enharmonic changes.]*

To remind you of what wonderful effects are attainable by the practical application of this artifice, let me quote a well-known passage from Beethoven's Sonate Pathétique, where, in the key of G minor, there occurs an inversion of the chord of the dominant minor 9th, which is resolved upon the chord of the tonic; the phrase is repeated, when the ♭E is changed to ♯D, B thus becomes the root of the chord and the key is accordingly changed to E minor. I wish you especially to notice the resolution of the C, which, by means of the enharmonic alteration, has become the minor 9th of B, the root of the altered chord. One may compare the strange and totally new sensation one experiences at the unexpected resolution of this single note consequent upon the enharmonic change, with what would be felt at the sudden illumination of a darkened chamber,—at the admission of the pure air of heaven into the long closed cell of a captive,— at the receipt of unlooked-for tidings by a care-worn and anxious heart.

Allow me to confirm whatever impression this last extract may have made upon you, by one other quotation from the same master which cannot be more wondrously beautiful, but is perhaps, from the greater prolongation of the several harmonies, more strikingly obvious. In this, the inversion of the tonic minor 9th of A is resolved at its repetition as though C were its root. To those who turn to the passage on paper, it may be as well to explain that, though, for convenience, the notation of C is unchanged, this note is resolved as ♭D, the 9th of C, when the supposed ♭D descends to C, the root of the altered chord, and the whole harmony is then resolved upon the new tonic of F. Can you picture one who has long lain in a hopeful dream, who yearns for happiness he has never known and so cannot define, awakening to learn that his dreaming is fulfilled, and to find the fact wholly unlike, yet a thousandfold lovelier than his expectation? Such a picture is realized in the remarkable passage before us ; a traveller who dreams of the home he is approaching, and wakes to find caressing friends around him looking the welcome of affection; an artist who dreams of the completion of his work, and wakes to witness its admiring reception by an appreciating public. Fancies such as these are quickly prompted by the exquisite passage to which I refer; but no thought of tangible form can represent its loveliness, no verbal language can translate its expression.

SYMPHONY IN A.—*Beethoven.*

Let us track out to their full extent the enharmonic resources, universal they may truly be called, of the inversions of a chord of the minor 9th. The chord

Modulation into 24 keys, by alterations of one chord.

as first written, in the following example, claims G for its root, counting upwards from which, the notes all stand at the interval of a 3rd apart. The change of ♭A to ♯G alters the highest 3rd into an augmented 2nd, and E thus becomes the root. The change of F to ♯E alters the next 3rd into an augmented 2nd, and ♯C then becomes the root. The restoration of the two highest notes with the change of B to ♭C, when the lowest third is altered into an augmented 2nd, gives us the chord of which ♭B is the root.

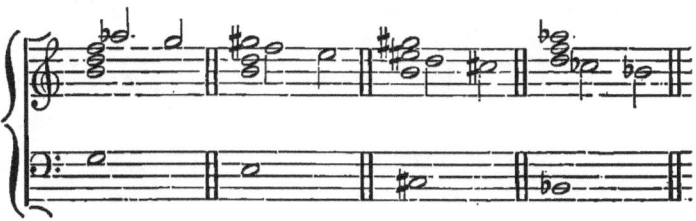

Please to observe that, in each of these differently noted chords, there are two notes next each other in alphabetical order—♭A B in the first, F ♯G in the second, D ♯E in the third, and ♭C D in the fourth chord. That one of the two which is lower in alphabetical order is, in each case, the minor 9th; and the root of the chord is always one semitone below it.

As the chord of the minor 9th of the dominant is precisely imitated, by means of chromatic notes, upon the supertonic and upon the tonic, and as the intervals in these three chords are identical, any chord of the minor 9th may be accounted either the dominant of one key, or the supertonic of another, or the tonic of yet another. An inversion of a chord of the minor 9th, you have seen, may be derived, according to enharmonic changes in its notation, from either of four roots. Each root may be either a dominant, or a supertonic, or a tonic. The inverted or incomplete chord may thus belong to either of three times four keys. The chords of the minor 9th are available indifferently in both minor and major keys. There are thus twice twelve keys into which every inverted chord of the minor 9th may be resolved; and, as there are but twelve sounds producible upon the pianoforte key-board, each of which may be the key-note of either a minor key or a major; these twenty-four major and minor keys are all the keys that exist in practical music. It has been shown, in the accompaniment of the chromatic scale with inversions of minor 9ths,* that there are three of these chords in a key; which of the three be dominant, which supertonic, and which tonic, is shown by the notation of the whole; and certainly every inversion of the chord of the minor 9th that can be written belongs, and must belong, to one of these three roots in some key or other.

We all remember the Arabian tale of the princess who was to be given in marriage to one of three brothers who could bring the rarest and most valuable treasure as the price of her hand; and of Prince Houssain, who fairly won the bride by the production of a wonderful carpet, which had the magical power

---

* Page 140.

to transport whoever sat upon it, instantaneously, to any place in the known or unknown world he wished to visit. Steam and electricity emulate in vain the locomotive power of the marvellous carpet; but what express trains and even telegraphs fail to accomplish, all these fairy wonders are achieved by this one chord. Literally, with the speed of thought, it is the means of modulation from any one key into every other; and the artist's imagination cannot so quickly conceive a transition from key to key, however extraneous, but that this miracle-working harmony as quickly effects the tonal translocation. The inverted chord of the minor 9th—the chord, that is, of the so-called diminished 7th—is, in fact, everywhere at once, and hence may be cited as the prosopopœia of ubiquity.

I throw myself on your patience while I exemplify this boundless modulative power in the chord we have been considering, by a series of transitions, from one commencement in the key of C, into every other key in music; but, not to tax that patience too severely, I will chose the twelve major keys only, leaving to your reflective powers the application of the same process to the minor form of the same tonics.

THE MODERN STYLE.

Or, in F. Or, in G.

Or, in A. Or, in D.

Or, in E.

Or, in ♯F.

THE MODERN STYLE.

Or, in B.

Or, in ♯C.

Or, in ♭E.   Or, in ♭A,

Or, in ♭B.

LECTURE V.

THE MODERN STYLE—*continued*.

IT is now to compare the beautiful and, one may call it, Protean chord of the minor 9th, described last week, with the analogous but strikingly different chord of the major 9th. But first we must mark that, while the major 3rd, the perfect 5th, and minor 7th in all fundamental discords are invariable ; the 9th may, at a composer's discretion, be either minor or major. This rule has, however, one important reservation ; namely, that the use of chords of the minor 9th is common to both minor and major keys, but that of chords of the major 9th— of the dominant and supertonic at least—is restricted to major keys. Here you will call to mind what was said of chromatic concords, that the diatonic harmonies of the minor key were chromatically available in the major, but that the diatonic harmonies of the major key were peculiar to it, and were not, and could not be, employed in the minor ;* and you will perceive that the speciality of the major 9th to the major key is a continuance of the same principle. Chords of the major 9th.

    The same rules for its resolution, either on the 8th or the 3rd of the same chord, govern the major as the Resolved on a note of the same chord.

---

* Page 116.

minor 9th. My wish is to prove these rules by their application, and to familiarize you with their working by demonstrating its effect, rather than to trouble you more than possible with purely technical details; I will therefore cite a passage, wherein a succession of major 9ths resolved on their roots has a sound of delicacy and intensity that must charm all hearers;

OBERON.—*Weber*.

and another, in which the character of the major 9th is happily contrasted with that of the minor under the same circumstances of approach and resolution, the minor 9th appearing in the first bar, and the major 9th in each of the three that follow, whose hopefulness of expression breaks beautifully out of the anxiety that precedes.

ZEMIRE UND AZOR.—*Spohr.*

This note, the major 9th, seems truly to glitter, for all its delicate softness, when it appears in a modification of the theme. I quoted last week from the final movement of Beethoven's Concerto in C minor, to exemplify the resolution of the minor 9th upon its 3rd,[*] the brightness of the altered phrase being singularly manifest from its contrast to the original.

The ascent instead of descent of the 9th to its 3rd, and the beauty of this progression, may be shown in a

---

[*] Page 136.

melody that loses none of its merits through its immense popularity, and that will be all the more readily remembered as an instance, because it is so universally known apart from this theoretical definition.

BOHEMIAN GIRL.—*Balfe.*
When o - ther lips and o - ther hearts

It is less rare with the major than the minor 9th, to write the root in substitution for the 7th, and to make it fall to the 7th while the 9th proceeds to the 3rd.

VIOLIN QUARTET, Op. 41.—*Schumann.*

SONATA, Op. 42.—*Schubert.*

This treatment gives singular prominence to the root, when it assumes somewhat of the poignancy of a discord, which, anomalously, one is disposed to fancy, is softened by the progression of the really consonant root to its dissonant 7th. Strangely, however, as discord and concord seem here to shift places and responsibilities, the genuine character of the 7th and root remains unchanged in relation to the complete harmony, and in reference to the demand of the 7th for ultimate resolution.

I know nothing sweeter, fonder, more tender in its expression, than the chord of the dominant major 9th when it is resolved upon the tonic harmony; listen to these striking illustrations. *Resolved on a note of another chord.*

VIOLIN SONATA.—*Mozart.*

VARIATIONS, Op. 82.—*Mendelssohn.*

DON GIOVANNI.—*Mozart.*

Supertonic major 9th.

Less frequent far in its use than that of the dominant is the chord of the supertonic major 9th; but its effect is so large, so mysterious, so sanguine, that each instance of its occurrence might well stamp itself as an indelible sign of beauty upon the memory. This is one of the harmonies, others of which I shall have opportunity to notice, that have been employed with such conspicuous good effect by Mendelssohn that they bring his name into our thoughts almost whenever we hear them; to exemplify its effect, however, I will take some passages from other composers, and thus show that living musicians may write the chord without meriting the aspersion that they borrow from the author of "Elijah." The resolution of the chord either upon that of the tonic or of the dominant, identifies it with the supertonic as its root, and you will feel that in the following quotations there is no hint of departure from the prevailing key.

THE MODERN STYLE. 161

ISRAEL.—*Handel.*

Idem.

LIEBESBOTSCHAFT.—*Schubert.*

162 *THE MODERN STYLE.*

Tonic Major 9th. Still more rare, but no less beautiful, is the employment of the chord of the tonic major 9th, which is distinguished by its resolution—with the chromatic progression of its 7th to the 3rd in the following harmony—upon a dominant discord, when the dissonance of the 9th is dissolved, so to speak, in the consonance of the dominant 5th.

Dominant 11th. The next interval of the harmonic series that comes under consideration is the 11th. This note is added to the chord of either the minor or major 9th, as the 9th is added to the chord of the 7th, and as the 7th is added to the common chord. It is not to be supposed that the whole six notes of this harmony ever are or can be sounded together, there is ample provision against such cacophony in the rule that forbids the sounding of a dissonance together with the note on which it is to be resolved, and in the rule that prohibits the progression to the unison or 8th, by oblique motion, of two notes next each other in alphabetical order. The same law excludes the root from the upper parts of the harmony when the 9th is resolved upon this note, and excludes the 3rd from the chord when the 9th is resolved upon it. There will nevetheless appear sufficient proof that the 11th is a generated note of a fundamental chord of which the dominant is the root, in the fully satisfactory effect of this said dominant, when played below all the available notes of the harmony, as the basis of the entire combination.

Like the 9th, either minor or major, as distinguished from the 7th, 5th, and 3rd, the 11th is often resolved on a note derived from its own root. It then proceeds to the 3rd, which therefore may not be sounded together with the 11th, while the 9th proceeds to the root, which therefore (except as the bass note) may not be sounded together with the 9th. *Resolved on a note of the same chord.*

Here, the 11th and 9th have a little the look of the diatonic double suspension of the 4th and 9th.* That these notes are not suspensions is proved, however, by their not being suspended, or prepared; and the chromatic approach to the unprepared 7th, in the above example, further conduces to the fundamental character of the whole harmony.

In the inversions of this chord, the presence of the 9th excludes the root, as has already been shown. There being then no sounded note with which the 7th forms a dissonance, in the absence of both the

---

* Page 72.

root and the 3rd of the chord, the 7th has no longer any of its septimal characteristics, but is, like the same interval in the inversions of the diatonic chord of the essential 9th,[a] free in its progression.

A MIDSUMMER NIGHT'S DREAM.—*Mendelssohn.*

The chord here bears somewhat the aspect of a diatonic 7th of which the supertonic would be the root.[b] That it is not this, is now shown by the non-preparation of either the 7th or the diminished 5th; whereas preparation is an exceptionless exaction of the strict style for all the discords it includes; and that it is not so, will be further established when I point out some other resolutions of the chord of the 11th, which are quite at variance with ancient strict regulation.

A rule that permits the leap of an augmented interval in melody—otherwise offensive and consequently disallowed—when the notes, to and from which the leap is made, belong to the same chord, may be adduced to confirm the derivation of the 11th as well as the 9th from the same root as the notes whence they are approached, and whereon they are

---

[a] Page 80. [b] Page 78.

resolved ; witness the following example, wherein so far from an offence to the ear, the leap of the augmented 2nd is a point of natural and therefore quite agreeable progression.

LA SONNAMBULA.—*Bellini.*

The 11th also rises to the 5th of its own root when the 9th rises to the 3rd.

That the resolution of these two notes is variable, disproves their control by the unexceptional rules of the strict style, and thus gives further evidence of their fundamental derivation ; and that they both rise with excellent effect to their resolution, fully establishes their government by a law distinct from that for the treatment of prepared discords. When, in the bass, the 5th of this chord proceeds to the root, the harmony with its progression still wears much of the aspect of an essential 7th of the strict style.[*] I will justify the word wears, by showing that such an aspect is not true to the chord, but an assumption

---

[*] Page 78.

founded on the momentary circumstances of its situation, and licensed by the prejudices of our early education. The 7th, 5th, and 3rd from the bass, in this inversion of the chord, are respectively the 11th, 9th, and 7th from the root. The non-preparation of the 7th from the bass separates the chord from the class of prepared discords; the minority of its 3rd distinguishes it from the chromatic chord of the supertonic 7th peculiar to the modern free style, which is known by its major 3rd; and the ascent of its 7th, with good effect, to the 5th in the ensuing form of the harmony, shows this note to be either no 7th at all, or else a 7th whose resolution is directed by a special rule individual to itself, an exception from exceptions.

SEHNSUCHT, Op. 51.—*Schumann.*

THE MODERN STYLE.

Now it is far simpler to regard this note as an 11th, whose treatment is analogous to that of the 9th,—as an 11th, whose existence is an expansion of, not a dereliction from, the principles already accepted,—than to consider it as forming a combination apart from all other chords in its constitution and in its resolution. The seemingly rootless harmony of the 3rd and 6th of the supertonic, that questionable concord of the strict style, has been satisfactorily traced to the dominant as its generator.[a] The analogous chord of the 3rd and 6th of the subdominant in a minor key, comprising the diminished 5th that lies between the 2nd and the minor 6th of the scale, is not otherwise accountable than as an incomplete form of the dominant minor 9th whose root and 3rd are therein omitted.[b] The so-called chord of the diminished 7th has been freely accepted by most modern theorists as an incomplete chord of the minor 9th.[c] The inversions of the chord of the major 9th whence the root is omitted, are no longer disputed to be such.[d] There needs then only to apply to the chord of the 11th the same process for tracing its root that was applied to the fundamental chords of the 9th and of the 7th, and the same reasoning in support of this, and every one must be convinced that the admission of the new element of the 11th is but a further development of an established principle; it is but to descend by 3rds from any note of the chord, until we reach a note whose perfect 5th is in the chord, whose major 3rd is

---

[a] Pages 52 and 103.   [b] Page 114.   [c] Page 138.   [d] Page 159.

not chromatically contradicted, and from which there is no interval of even number, and this note is the root of the entire harmony.

The accompaniment of the 9th with the root instead of the 7th, and the progression of this root to its 7th when the 9th is resolved on its 3rd,[a] sometimes occurs when the 11th also is in the chord and proceeds to the 5th, as I have just described, together with the resolution of the 9th. There is a beautiful instance of this very modern progression in Mendelssohn's Overture to *A Midsummer Night's Dream*, that marvellous work of a stripling, which contains more previously unwritten harmonic effects than I believe any piece in existence; it introduced to the world indeed so much that was novel, yet beautiful as new, that it may be esteemed an inspired revelation of some natural truths uttered in the spiritual language of the ideal.

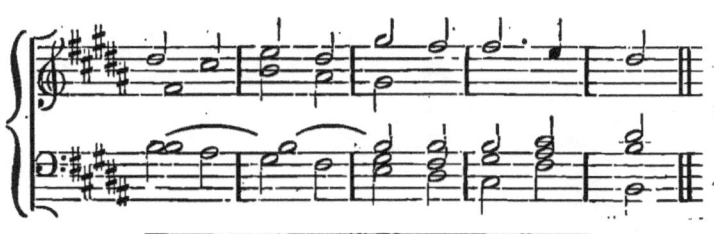

[a] Page 158.

Beyond what I have already shown, the ♯F, in the chord I now notify, is further evidence of the source of the harmony; since, were this note the suspended 4th of its ♯C bass, it should proceed as a dissonance to the 3rd of such bass, whereas, being truly the most consonant note in the combination, its progression to the dissonant 7th in the ensuing form of the chord is perfectly natural.

The chord of the 11th is peculiar to the dominant; since, if derived from any other root than this, it cannot be satisfactorily resolved within the key, the 11th itself being indeed the key-note, wherever the context proves it to be an 11th. The natural resolution of this chord upon one derived from another root is when it proceeds to the chord of the key-note. Nothing is more familiar, and nothing more satisfactory than the resolution of an inverted chord of the 11th upon the 2nd inversion of the key-note;

<small>Resolved on a note of another chord.</small>

VIOLIN QUARTET IN ♭E.—*Mozart.*

and nothing further than this can, I think, be needed to exemplify the exceptional character of the harmony. Rameau, the distinguished French composer, at the beginning of the eighteenth century, defines the chord, in this position and with this resolution, as the chord of the added 6th, meaning thereby that it consists of a 6th added to the common chord of the subdominant. It is not my purpose to show you what chords are not, but what they are; neither would I willingly merit the character of a controversialist; I shall therefore not trouble you with arguments to refute the theory of Rameau; but I have thus far alluded to it, in order that, should you meet with mention of the chord under his designation, you may know it to be this same we are now considering.

A remarkably bold and broad effect is produced by the progression of the 7th—the bass note in this inversion of the chord—to the root of the tonic harmony, a progression justified by the absence of both the notes with which the 7th would form a dissonance requiring resolution. A grand application of this occurs in the interludes of the Choral, "Sleepers wake," in Mendelssohn's *St. Paul;* and I might refer you to many others, more or less striking, in the works of the same composer, the frequency of which brings the treatment of the chord under consideration to be sometimes regarded as peculiar to him.

This particular passage has been the subject of great theoretical discussion, and it has been the most warmly discussed by those who have admired it most; but I can find no other explanation satisfactory than this I have given you—namely, that G, the enfranchised 7th, proceeds to D, the root of the tonic chord; B, the 9th, proceeds to A its 5th; E, the always free 5th, proceeds to ♯F its 3rd; and D, the 11th, remains to double the tonic root.

In so far as fact is more forcible than argument, the excellently good effect of the chord of the 11th with the root as its bass note, must be still more convincing that this bass is its root, than any of the suggestions, however strong, that I have shown to be prompted by the special sound of the inverted forms of the chord, or by the analogy of these to other fundamental harmonies. The good effect to which I refer is but seldom to be found I own; but, to select from others one most powerful example, let me direct your attention to its employment at the culminating note of a phrase in the overture to Schumann's Opera, *Genoveva*, that derives more prominence, more intensity, and indeed I may say more beauty, from its accompaniment by this chord, than any other harmony could impart to it.

Besides its resolution upon the chord of the keynote, the chord of the 11th is also often resolved upon a supertonic discord.

REQUIEM.—*Mozart.*

pec - ca - ta   mun - di.

It may be esteemed an act of art heroism to have opened a composition with this then unlicensed discord; and musicians may fitly thank as much the daring as the genius of Beethoven, not only for having forefelt what theoretical analysis has since fathomed, the speciality of this chord of the 11th, but for having defied orthodoxy by his employment of the harmony in a situation and in a manner that make its use most bold and most uncompromising. The temerity of the master is nobly repaid by the unprecedented and, truly, speaking expression with which this initial chord characterizes his whole movement; notice how the stern, rugged air of the commencement, softens at the change of harmony until it gives place to playful sweetness at the full close of the theme.

SONATA, No. 3, Op. 29 (or 31).—*Beethoven.*

The infinite range of modulation by means of enharmonic changes of the inversions of the minor 9th, is not to be paralleled by the treatment of any other harmony. It is at least analogous to this manifold interpretation of one combination of sounds—this punning, one may call it, upon a chord—however, that the chord of the 11th in one key, with its root and 3rd omitted, is composed of the same notes as the chord of the major 9th in another key, with its root only omitted; and that either of these, however approached, may be resolved, according to its derivation from the alternative root, into the other key.

Modulation by the chord, of the 11th.

Dominant minor 13th. The minor 13th is the note that next follows the 11th in the available harmonic series. It is added to the chord of the 11th, as the 11th, minor or major 9th, and 7th, were successively added to the common chord in the building up of this column of sound.

Some opponents of the theory I am unfolding to you, from the knowledge of which I have experienced unlimited practical advantage,—some opponents of these views have thought to overturn them by humorously defining the chord of the 13th as a combination of the entire seven notes of the scale—an incongruous abomination such as no ear could tolerate. The joke is well sounding; it is so probably because of its hollowness. The stringent rule against the simultaneous striking of a dissonance with the note of its resolution precludes either the root or the 3rd from a chord of the 9th, either the 3rd or the 5th when the 11th is added to this, and either the 5th or 7th when the 13th is superadded. Here then is sure safeguard for the protection of oral sensitiveness from the outrageous intrusion of three out of the seven notes; and you will find that the chord of the 13th of practical use —like those of the 11th and of the 9th—generally comprises but a selection of its constituent sounds. For all that may be said by scoffers, however, there are instances of the effective employment of the chord in its entirety; and, not to adduce a lesser authority, I will refer you to the passage introducing the first vocal solo in the choral movement in Beethoven's last symphony—not as a specimen of harmonious sweetness indeed, but as a living proof that the combination is tolerable, and, where it occurs, is the best possible expression of the composer's thought.

The minor 13th is sometimes resolved on the 7th of its own root. *Resolved on a note of the same chord.*

It is resolved far more frequently upon its 5th; when, for the most part, it is accompanied with no other note than the root, the 3rd and the 7th, but sometimes also with the 9th. You must feel, as every composer that has written it must have felt, how tender, how far more pathetic than any interval in harmony, is the note in question.

QUARTET IN C MINOR, Op. 18.—*Beethoven.*

QUARTET IN F, Op. 18.—*Beethoven.*

Of the two examples in the former of these extracts, the first, the 13th of G, appears upon a tonic pedal; the second, the 13th of C, has its root in the bass. The latter extract shows the 13th together with the root, 3rd, 7th, and 9th.

Some disputants of this theory have sought to include the 13th, when thus resolved, in the category of suspensions. The fallacy of their view is established in the fact that the note needs no preparation—nay, that its beauty is often best revealed when it is approached by leap either from an interval of the same or of another chord. Further, the 13th is peculiar to the three available roots of fundamental discords; whereas all suspensions or their inversions are common to every note in the key.

The more incomplete chord consisting of the minor 13th, 3rd, and doubled root, looks more simple than that we have just examined; but it has this somewhat greater complexity in its treatment, that, as it is unsatisfactory for the 13th to pass away and leave a vague consonant harmony, the root must proceed to the 7th when the 13th resolves upon the 5th, so as to supply still a dissonance demanding definite resolution.

QUARTET IN C MINOR, Op. 18.—*Beethoven.*

The liberation of the 7th by the omission of the notes with which this one forms a dissonance has already been seen.* The minor 9th, 11th, and minor 13th—each resolved on the note below it—are written with the 7th, which freely rises to its root when the other three notes descend to the root, 3rd, and 5th.

---

* Page 164.

You cannot but notice the force while you admit the delicacy of this form of the chord as it occurs in the following passage.

DER FREYSCHÜTZ.—*Weber.*

Resolved on a note of another chord.

When resolved on a chord derived from another root, the chord of the dominant minor 13th follows the natural course of all the other harmonies generated by the dominant, in proceeding to the chord of the tonic. The interval of the minor 13th then remains to be the minor 3rd of the tonic, just as the minor 9th of the supertonic (the diminished 7th from the augmented 4th of the key[a]) remains to be the minor 3rd in the common chord of the key-note. With this resolution the chord is most frequently employed in its last inversion—having, that is, the 13th in the bass, it is however also sometimes written with its root in the bass, of which form, as well as the other, I shall presently give you an instance. Among recent composers, no one has employed the chord we are now discussing with better effect, and perhaps more frequently, than Mendelssohn; but I prefer to illustrate its remarkable beauty, its profound

---

[a] Page 142.

richness of tone, and its wonderful depth of pathos, by some passages from that extraordinary anticipation of modern resources, that prophecy of all that is accomplished in the music of the present and all that can be possible in the music of the future, the Chromatic Fantasia of Sebastian Bach, rather than cite examples from the writings of any of the later masters who have been as proud to avow how much they have owed to the study of their giant predecessor, as they have been quick to perceive the minuteness and the vastness of his all-grasping genius.

I must here revert to a passage in the second of these lectures, wherein the suspension of the augmented 5th over the 3rd of a minor key was examined.* I spoke then of the unique effect of this

---

* Page 70.

discord in diatonic harmony, of its singular poignancy, and of its suggesting much of the feeling of modern music when and wherever it might be heard. This harmony—strictly a suspension when prepared and resolved according to the laws of the diatonic style—is identical with the chord we are now considering, the last inversion of the minor 13th, in which the augmented 5th from the bass is the inverted 3rd of the entire chord; and the chord of the key-note which follows the dominant discord, is identical with the resolution of the diatonic suspension. I shall later have to show that all the harmonies of the ancient style which are distinguished by any peculiar or exceptive interval, find their full explanation in the principles of our modern fundamental chords; but I here specially direct attention to the identity of this one chord in the two systems, because I feel that the different rules of its application in the ancient and modern styles throw each a light upon the other.

So far as has yet been explained, the use of the interval of the minor 13th is limited to minor keys. Its effect is notably different, and its expression is reversed from pain to delight, when it is used in major keys. It cannot then be resolved on a note derived from its own root. In proceeding to the chord of the key-note, the minor 13th of the dominant rises chromatically, like the minor 9th of the supertonic, to the major 3rd of the following chord.

VIOLIN QUARTET, No. 4, IN ♭E.—*Mozart.*

Gentle sweetness with earnest longing is embodied in this quotation, and a like expression marks many another phrase wherein the same chord is similarly employed. Its use is not less appropriate to the utterance of fiery eagerness, or all-mastering determination, dependent on the context, on the character of the entire passage to which it is incidental, for its various significance of tenderness or vehemence. Notice what rapturous excitement this chord under consideration gives to the rushing climax, which leads to the re-entry of the chief subject and the original key of the movement of the symphonic Allegro of Mendelssohn's *Hymn of Praise.*

The expedient false notation on which I have several times dilated, is exemplified in the two last extracts, where the minor 13th is written as an

False notation of minor 13th.

---

* Radically ♭F, not ♮F.   ᵇ Radically ♭G, not ♯F.
        ᶜ Radically ♭D, not ♯C.

augmented 5th from the root. That it is such, and that it should be so written, are insisted upon by many eminent theorists; truth is the only obstacle to the former proposition, expediency is the sole justification of the latter.

<small>Augmented Minor 13th.</small> A like looking chord to this, when written as an augmented 5th, and to a certain extent a like progressing one, is the essential discord of the augmented 5th on the mediant of a minor key, peculiar to the diatonic style.[a] Call to mind what has been more than once advanced as to the different sound of any pianoforte key when struck under different circumstances of tonality; listen to two phrases wherein this disputed chord is severally written, according to the key in which it occurs, with ♯D and ♭E; and decide, not in deference to me, but in obedience to your own conviction, whether or not the said pianoforte key give you in the two cases the same impression. The first phrase shall be in the key of E minor, of which ♯D is the diatonic leading-note, when B, the dominant, freely descends to the fifth of the next chord; the second in the key of C, of which ♭E is the chromatic minor 3rd, when B, then the leading-note, imperatively rises to the root of the tonic harmony.

[a] Page 75.

This test, you will recollect, was applied to the true and the expedient notations of the inversions of the supertonic minor 9th;[*] it may here be extended by the addition of another part to the harmony, which part shall contain the 7th in the questioned chord, such 7th being major when duly prepared in the key of E minor, and being minor when freely approached without preparation in the key of C.

If this fail to satisfy the most obstinate sceptic, I have reserved a proof that must batter down every opposition but that of wilful prejudice or the irretractability of a once spoken word. It is undoubted that the natural and sharp forms of a note cannot co-exist in a chord; I speak not of chromatic passing notes, which, as almost every page of modern music bears evidence, may be written with good effect together with the diatonic notes, essential to the harmony, of which they are the modification; when therefore you hear our old second phrase, with the addition of yet another part containing the 5th of the questioned chord, when you hear ♮D precluding the co-existence of ♯D as an essential note of the same harmony, and hear that—however rare its use, however extreme its

---
[*] Page 145.

effect—the chord is tolerable to your oral sense, you must admit that its derivation from the dominant is reasonable to your intellectual understanding, and that, being thence derived, ♭E must be the name of the doubted note.

Opponents to the theory of the minor 13th have yet an argument to which every enthusiast whose organ of veneration is developed must succumb. To write the note as the flat of that on whose natural form it is to resolve, as ♭E ♮E, they say is contrary to the practice of the great masters. I will withhold what might be urged against this statement, were it not my task to impeach the statement itself; since it might seem wanton both to annul the argument and to prove its impotency, to kill and then to hang it in chains. I have shown that Mozart and Mendelssohn have written the minor 13th as an augmented 5th, and I could show you countless like instances in the music of other authors; I have also shown, in last week's lecture, that it has not been uncommon for the great masters to write the inversions of the minor 9th with similarly expedient false notation;[a] I have now

---

[a] Page 143.

only to show that best approved musicians have written the minor 13th as a 13th, and thus established that, as in the case of the minor 9th, their practice is variable, and an equal authority, at least, for one view of the subject and for the other. Two instances will serve the purpose as well as two thousand, and these I draw at random from the works of a living and of a dead composer. In the Caprice for pianoforte and orchestra of Professor Sterndale Bennett, one of his most individual and admirable compositions, produced when his powers were quite matured, appears the following, with ♮G not ×F.

In Beethoven's great violin quartet in ♭B, one of his latest compositions, produced after a ceaselessly active life's experience, appears the following with ♭♭B: not ♮A.

QUARTET, Op. 130.—*Beethoven.*

THE MODERN STYLE.

Supertonic minor 13th. The chord of the supertonic minor 13th is of infrequent occurrence. Having detained you thus long with the investigation of a matter to which less rarity gives greater consequence, I will therefore but briefly exemplify the principal resolutions of this chord, in order to show that it holds its place in the harmonic or fundamental series.

Tonic minor 13th. The chord of the tonic minor 13th is more often written; and it may be distinguished by its progression to either a dominant or a supertonic discord.

It is not uncommon for it to be also resolved upon the harmony of the subdominant, when the implied modulation into the key of which this note is the tonic is falsified by the immediate succession of harmonies peculiar to the original key of the passage wherein the chord with this resolution appears.

DIE LOTUSBLUME.—*Schumann.*

The inversions of a chord of the minor 9th, you must recollect from last week's exemplification, comprise four notes which stand at the interval of minor 3rd or augmented 2nd each above the other; every one of these four is subject to enharmonic change, according to which, either of four notes not sounded in the chord may be its root; and each of these roots may be the dominant, or the supertonic, or the tonic of a key, the relation of the root to which key is determined by the resolution of the chord. In like manner, though not to equal extent, are the inversions of an incomplete chord of the minor 13th subject to enharmonic metamorphoses. The minor 13th, the root, and the 3rd stand at ascending intervals of major 3rds; either of these notes being

Enharmonic changes of minor 13th.

---

* Radically ♭D, not ♯C.

enharmonically changed, the major 3rd between it and the next note in the chord becomes a diminished 4th, and the root is altered accordingly. In the following table, the chord first appears as that of the augmented 5th proper, the mediant of E minor, the original 13th, being then its bass, while B is its fundamental root; it next appears with its root in the bass, ♭E being then the 13th; and it lastly appears with its 3rd in the bass, when ♭E is its root, and ♭C the minor 13th.

B   G   ♭E

Modulation into 18 keys by alterations of one chord.

It is understood that each of these roots, B, G, and ♭E, may be either of the three generators whose harmonics are practically available in composition— a dominant, a supertonic, or a tonic. Multiplying three roots, by three possible relationships to a key, we have hence nine minor keys and nine major, into which this one combination of sounds may discretionally be resolved.

Give me your patient indulgence while I demonstrate this changeful power of the chord of the minor 13th by a series of varied endings, in nine major keys, of one always repeated beginning of a phrase in the key of C; your own powers of reflection and comparison will assure you that a similar process would lead with satisfactory effect to the nine minor keys of the same tonics.

THE MODERN STYLE.

THE MODERN STYLE.

Or, in B.

Or, in ♭A.

Or, in ♭D.

Or, in ♭E.

LECTURE VI.

THE MODERN STYLE—*concluded*.

THE chord of the major 13th may be registered as Dominant
major 13th. the sister of the minor 13th described last week; and a fair parallel may be drawn between these two harmonies, with one source but with diverse characters, and the two sisters in Scott's romance; Minna, whose life and whose love are coloured with sadness, and Brenda, whose gay and truthful existence sparkles in the sunshine of her own creation; this, a carcanet of smiles, the other a rosary of tears. You will recollect the resemblance, the almost sameness of treatment, and the great disparity of effect between the minor and the major 9th; and a comparison of those chords with these of the 13th will help to a clear conception of the nature of both.

Like the interval of the minor 13th, the major is Resolved on
a note of the
same chord. sometimes resolved with charming effect upon its own 7th.

QUARTET IN ♭B, Op. 130.—*Beethoven*.

The interval of the major 13th, again like the minor, is also resolved, and far more frequently than on any other note, upon its own 5th.

VIOLIN SONATA IN A, Op. 12.—*Beethoven.*

Here, the chord being in its first inversion, how tender, yet how exquisitely bright is the large full meaning of the dissonant note; it seems a tear of joy through which the lustre of the eye shines with tenfold radiance.

PIANOFORTE SONATA, Op. 125.—*Spohr.*

Here, the chord having once its 7th, and once its root in the bass, the melodious context gives another expression to the harmony we are considering, all of which it takes back into itself, being enriched by its own liberality.

SYMPHONY IN D MINOR, Op. 49.—*Spohr.*

Here, the chords of the minor and of the major 13th occur in alternate phrases, the first three in the keys of ♭B, C minor and ♭E, being taken on tonic pedals, the fourth, in the key of C minor, having its root in the bass; and the passage illustrates, and I think justifies, the different character of expression I have ascribed to the two chords.

A more complete form of the chord, including the 11th, the 9th, the root in place of the 7th (as it was employed with the 9th only, and with the 9th and 11th[*]), together with the 5th as the bass note, occurs

---

[*] Page 168.

with admirable effect in the following phrase, where it proceeds to the more simple chord of the 7th derived from its own root. No satisfactory, no plausible account can be given of this remarkable yet truly beautiful combination and progression, other than the explanation I have offered; but whoever hears and feels the powerful significance of the harmony, must honour the theorist whose principles prove its derivation.

OVERTURE TO ATHALIE.—*Mendelssohn.*

<small>Supertonic major 13th.</small> The examples already given are of the dominant major 13th. Much more rarely but, possibly on this account, with even more intensity, is the supertonic major 13th employed; let me instance a prominent passage in Schumann's pianoforte trio in D minor, where the note in question appears to quiver for its moment of life with a rapture so keen, while so delicate, that nothing else could give it utterance.

In this passage the 13th is accompanied with its 3rd and its minor 9th; the expedient false notation of this 9th (written ♯G instead of ♭A), disguises the chord, giving it the appearance of a derivative of E; the same appearance is presented by the harmony with ♯G in the bass, two bars earlier in the passage, which is an inversion of the supertonic 9th in the key of F, as is proved by its resolution, and by the effect of unbroken continuity of key, in spite of the two chords being dressed in the notation of another tonality.

The tonic major 13th needs mention, but only to acknowledge its occasional use; its distinction from those of the dominant and the supertonic is to be traced through its relationship to the succeeding harmonies. *Tonic major 13th.*

It is not very common for the cord of the major 13th, belonging to whichever root, to be resolved on an entirely different chord. It is my object rather to help you to know harmonies of frequent occurrence in the writings of the best masters, to aid you to distinguish and again to recognise the resources of the greatest artists, than to lay before you a complete dictionary of chords wherein you might find an etymology, and a meaning for every combination in music. I will therefore not perplex your memory of the harmonies in general use which have been and are yet to be illustrated, by examples of this chord in its least familiar form. One only I must adduce, and that because of its unique effect and singular beauty. In Mozart's Fantasia in C minor you will find the following passage. *Resolved on a note of another chord.*

To borrow a term from the grammar of language, the first chord in the foregoing is thus to be parsed :—the bass part is an arpeggio of a portion of the harmony with an ornamental passing-note at the sixth quaver of the bar ; the virtual bass is then the first and last note of the bar, on which the harmony is attacked and quitted ; A, the bass note, is the major 13th of C, the dominant of F minor, and it is resolved on ♭A the 3rd of the tonic ; E is the 3rd in the dominant chord, the leading-note, and it is resolved on the key-note ; ♯C is so written for the expedient purpose of giving the chord familiar aspect, but it is truly ♭D, the minor 9th of the dominant, and it is resolved on the 5th of the tonic ; G is the 5th of the dominant, as a perfect interval it needs no resolution, and it might freely proceed to either note of the tonic chord. The same analysis applies to the transposed passage in the following bars. The chord, as Mozart spells it, looks like a chord of the 7th of which A is the root ; it sounds like nothing of the kind. This discrepancy between sound and sight results from the composer's complacency in dressing his chord in familiar intervals, so that it might pass unchallenged by the sentinels of conventionality ; while he knew that a chord of the 7th upon A had no more fitness in the key of F minor, than a phrase in his own German tongue would have in a Sanscrit poem; but he felt the eminent beauty of the progression, and its truthfulness to the tonality, and he imagined his music for the ears, though he wrote it for the eyes. I could confirm my views of the derivation of the chord, I could warrant the master in this its most striking application, by extracts from other composers where the same harmony was similarly treated; but I will trouble you with no more than one, which I choose as curiously showing how, a century sooner, the chord was written, with less courtesy to appearances, I believe, correctly; and as showing how the really great men of the transition period between the ancient style and the modern foresaw the discoveries of later times.

OVERTURE, BONDUCA.—*Purcell.*

All the chords as yet described may be classed as simple chords; for, however extreme the intervals which some of them comprise, these intervals are primary harmonics of the original roots. Each of these harmonics would in turn become the root of a harmonic series of its own, and hence the infinity of

Chords of the augmented 6th

the harmonic system of which I long since spoke. The 5th, being the note of next prominence to the generator in the harmonic series, is naturally the note whose harmonics are the most conspicuous after those of the primary root. These, the harmonics of the 5th, are taken in combination with certain notes peculiar to the primary root; but no other note than the 5th is, or can be, employed as a secondary root; since the harmonics of the 3rd, the 7th, and all the other intervals, comprise notes foreign to the tonality of the original generator.

We have now to consider what may be fitly classed as compound chords, the chords compounded of harmonics of a primary root with harmonics of its 5th, all of which include the interval of the augmented 6th, and all of which are designated by the name of this interval. The interval of the augumented 6th is greater by a semitone than the major 6th, as this is a semitone wider than the minor 6th.

It is to be found but twice only in the true chromatic scale, between the minor 2nd and the leading-note, and between the minor 6th and the augmented 4th.

This latter is, by very far, of more common occurrence than the other, and it demands therefore our chief attention.

The dominant gives out its minor 9th as a primary harmonic. The 5th of the dominant (the supertonic) gives out its major 3rd as a secondary harmonic.

On Minor 6th.

Between the minor 9th of the dominant and the major 3rd of the supertonic is the interval of the augmented 6th; which two notes, taken in combination, are accompanied with the 7th of the supertonic, either alone, or together with the root, or together with the minor 9th, these 7th, root, and 9th, being respectively the 3rd, 4th, and 5th from the lower note of the augmented 6th.

The three chords of the augmented 6th are often distinguished as the Italian, the French, and the German 6th. There may be a reason for this, in each chord having been first used among the musicians whose nationality defines it; but I have no evidence to support the supposition. One may fancy, however, something characteristic of the comparative softness of the Italian nature in the first chord, the piquancy of the French in the second chord, and the bold decision of the German in the third chord; and, merely fanciful though these characteristics be, if the sound of the notes in any degree accord with the suggestion, this may perhaps help to impress both the chord and its effect upon the memory.

In almost all cases the interval of the augmented 6th is resolved upon an octave, and this octave is either the root or the 5th of a chord. If the octave— which is the dominant—be the root of the resolving chord, this is of course major; and you will perceive with what ample sonority, with what truly large effect, a half close is approached from one of the chords of the augmented 6th.

VIOLIN SONATA, Op. 30.—*Beethoven.*

If the octave, whereupon the interval of the augmented 6th diverges, be the 5th of the chord, this chord is either minor or major, according to the key of the passage in which the chord of the augmented 6th with its resolution occurs. Observed how stern a grandeur is imparted to a full close in a minor key by its approach from this emphatic harmony.

SYMPHONY IN G MINOR.—*Mozart.*

And, again, notice how unwontedly bright sounds the inversion of the major tonic, when a chord of the augmented 6th precedes it.

SYMPHONY IN ♭B.—*Beethoven.*

202 THE MODERN STYLE.

The enharmonic change of the chord of the dominant 7th in the key of B, into the chord of the augmented 6th in the key of ♭B, gives to the resolution of this latter, in the passage just quoted, that magical effect which amazes at once and delights us with the beautiful affinity yet utter unlikeness of the two keys,—two families of sound, two different climates of tone, may I call them,—thus brought into opposition.

Inversion of augmented 6th. It is most rare for composers to invert the interval of the augmented 6th by placing the major 3rd of the secondary root below the minor 9th of the primary root, and thus producing the interval of the diminished 3rd.

The very infrequent use of this inversion is accountable by its extreme, nay, let me say its excessive, harshness. You may here recall my repeated observation of the different effect of any pianoforte key under different tonal relationship; which, as has more than once been shown, proves that the enharmonic diesis is not merely a technical puzzle resulting from several names of one sound, but that it distinguishes different keys and different harmonies; and proves also that the sensitive ear has the delicate capacity of discriminating the various effects of two notes represented by one pianoforte key. The last inversion of a chord of the dominant 7th in the key of ♭D having ♭G in the bass, has the root of the chord ♭A at the interval of a major 2nd—two semitones—above the bass ;

a discord undoubtedly this is, but, rough and rugged though it be, there is a noble frankness in its sound which befits it for hearty, large expression. In the key of C, the diminished 3rd from ♯F to ♭A—likewise two semitones—has an effect upon the hearer obviously different from that of the same pianoforte keys when sounded with a different context ;

here I feel the interval to be narrow, crushed in its character, and full of bitter complaining in its expression. Artists of lower rank, of small experience, or of extravagantly melodramatic aspiration, have written this chord more freely than would warrant what has just been said ; with the deference due to such composers, I must still aver that I feel the indiscreet use of so extreme a chord to be more free than welcome. In some few cases, however—so few that they may quickly be numbered, and so remarkable that any musician of moderate memory may point to them all—the inversion of the augmented

6th has been employed with exquisite fitness to a most intense expression, and with consequent beauty of effect. Let me instance a passage that has called forth many a comment, from Church musicians especially, a passage wherein this chord occurs with admirable pertinence, in the anthem, "Hear my crying," by John Weldon, a composer of the time of George I.

After nearly a century and a half—showing that the use of the chord was no more a barbarism of the elder time than an over-refinement of the modern—the same harmony was written, with I think the same expressive purpose, and with the same touching effect, by Mendelssohn, in his hymn *Hear my Prayer*.

On minor 2nd.

Though written but seldom, very seldom in comparison with those we have been considering, the chords of the augmented 6th upon the minor 2nd of the key are also employed with admirable effect, of which the following is a notable instance.

VIOLIN SONATA, Op. 30.—*Beethoven*.

The coda of the scherzo in Beethoven's Sonata in C, Op. 2, No. 3, presents examples of the chord of augmented 6th on the minor 6th of the key, and of that on the minor 2nd, in such immediate neighbourhood as to render comparison easy and obvious, of the different effects of the two.

I have stated generally, of the chromatic harmonies of the supertonic and of those of the tonic, that these are distinguished from chords of which the dominant is the root, by their not proceeding to a concord whose root is at the interval of a perfect 4th above their own. When the hearer's comprehension extends beyond the progression of one chord to the next, when it includes an entire musical sentence, and can perceive the relation of any chord to the sense of a complete phrase as affected by the context, many an instance will then be apparent of a chromatic supertonic harmony being followed by a concord of the dominant

Extended use of supertonic and tonic chromatic chords.

to induce a half-close, and many of a chromatic tonic discord being followed by a chord of the subdominant, when some chord especially characteristic of the key directly ensues—this latter being frequent in the case of a tonic pedal.

<small>Pedals in the free style.</small> In the modern style, pedal notes—notes that are continued through changing harmonies of which the pedal may or may not be an essential element—are governed by the same law that regulates their treatment in the ancient style, but the limits of its application are now greatly widened. The tonic and the dominant, and no other notes, are available as pedals; and while either, or even both of these notes are prolonged, any chords proper to the key of which the pedal is the tonic or the dominant, chromatic chords or diatonic, are employed with the same freedom and treated after the same rules as if the pedal were not present; in brief, any passage that quits not one key may have a tonic or dominant pedal sounded throughout its continuance. You may find almost as many examples of pedals as you may find pieces of music produced within the last hundred years; any one that would adequately represent the remarkable effect either of repose or of climax a pedal passage may produce would be too long to extract; let me refer you therefore, for notable illustration, to the tonic pedal in Mozart's Overture to Idomeneo, and to the dominant pedals in some of Handel's harpsichord Fugues, in the first chorus in Bach's wonderful setting of the Passion according to St. Matthew, in the coda of the opening Allegro Con Brio in Beethoven's Sin-

fonia Eroica (where the pedal note is alternated in the bass with other notes of the changing harmonies) and in the coda of the final presto in Mendelssohn's Octet.

The notes available as roots of fundamental chords are the tonic, the dominant (which is its 5th), and the supertonic (which is the 5th of the dominant). The submediant (which is the 5th of the supertonic) cannot be added to these, however sequent upon the course of ascension from 5th to 5th its introduction may appear. The submediant cannot be added to the number of the available fundamental roots, because its major 3rd—the note that especially characterizes all fundamental harmonies—would displace the keynote, and so change the key. The relation between any major key and the minor key of its supertonic is singularly intimate, so intimate that a modulation into this latter and a return to the original key scarcely disturb our sense of one prevailing tonality.

C   D minor.   C

This, I think, is explained by the notes of the minor supertonic triad being all traceable to the dominant as their generator, of which they are the 5th, 7th, and major 9th; just as the notes of the diminished supertonic triad—peculiar to the minor key, and chromatically written in the major[a]—are traceable to the dominant as its 5th, 7th, and minor 9th. It appears to be a consequence of the derivation of the minor supertonic triad from the dominant, that the fundamental harmonies of the submediant, including its major 3rd, if followed by this minor supertonic triad, are available upon a dominant pedal; that is, in the key of C, while the note G is continued, a chord of A major, a chord of the 7th of A, or a chord of the 9th of A, if followed by a chord containing ♮F, has an excellent effect which in no respect equivocates the permanence of C as the tonic, notwithstanding the C in the submediant chord. So far as I have been able to trace, Mozart was the first to show the availablity of this beautiful harmonic resource, and the following is a charming example of its application by him.

DIE ZAUBERFLÖTE.—*Mozart.*

ich wür-de wür-de &c.

Inverted Pedals.

The pedal note in modern music, somewhat in contradiction to its name, is often written with good effect in one of the upper parts in a score. That it is thus available, not only as the foot or bass of a

---

[a] Page 114.

series of changing harmonies, but as a note whose sound pierces through the midst or shines above them all, has been accounted for by the different qualities of tone of the several instruments of the orchestra. Quality is to some extent an equivalent for pitch; and the unlikeness, thus, of the tone of a trumpet to that of a violin, distinguishes as much the sound of these two instruments, and separates them as completely in effect, as though their notes were some octaves asunder. There is more than this, however, to be said in explanation of what has been called the inverted pedal—namely, the pedal above or in the midst of the harmony. The dominant and the tonic are notes of such paramount importance, are so inseparable from our sense of key, and so completely permeate—either in expressed sound or understood implication—all possible harmonies, that we can satisfactorily hear either of these continue in any position through a series of chords, provided only that it interfere not with the clearness of the part-writing. Most simply to exemplify this inverted pedal, let me turn to a passage where the dominant is continued in an inner part, while the quasi-modulation into the implied minor key of the supertonic takes place, of which I have just spoken; and you will hear that the continuance of the dominant is perfectly harmonious as regards each particular combination; and that as regards the general tone of effect, this continued dominant establishes such affinity between the supertonic with minor 3rd and the tonic, that we have no more impression of a change

P

of key in the passage now before us than we had in that of Mozart where the pedal was in the bass.

FIDELIO.—*Beethoven.*

The extreme limit of the availability of the fundamental harmonies of the submediant, is their employment upon a tonic pedal. This is a dangerous point on which to touch, since its fair discussion would far exceed all bounds of time at our present disposal, and of space too, if every argument were to be substantiated by a written quotation. I must content me then with the bare statement of the fact that the two greatest masters of modern musical art have written what I have here described, have written it with what is applauded as beautiful effect; and I leave the justification of such daring passages to other analysts, or at least till another opportunity.

OVERTURE, DON GIOVANNI.—*Mozart.*

SINFONIA EROICA.—*Beethoven.*

One matter more claims our notice before we quit our consideration of pedals. It is imperative that, whatever incongruity appear between the successive harmonies and the continuous pedal note, this note cannot be finally quitted except when it is an essential member of a chord. An effect, seemingly supernatural, and unsurpassably beautiful, has been produced by a change of key during the continuance of a certain note which has been long held as a dominant pedal and then becomes a minor 13th, bearing above it the other notes of the dominant harmony in the new key, and the bass note becomes the minor 3rd of the tonic chord when this dominant harmony of the new key is resolved upon it. The Scherzo of Schumann's Symphony in ♭E, and his Hochländisches Wiegenlied present very remarkable instances of this device, which also could not be more felicitously illustrated than by the following, a continuation of a dominant pedal.

VARIATIONS, Op. 82.—*Mendelssohn.*

Extended relationship of keys.

There is now to speak of the vastly extended range of keys that are brought into mutual relationship by the obvious and insoluble links of the chromatic genus. When it was first proved that those harmonies which were available as chromatic chords induced no modulation, when chromatic concords were first described, it was shown that all the diatonic harmonies peculiar to the minor key were chromatically available in the major—shown, in fact, that the major key included the minor.[a] This it does, not only as regards its resources of harmony, as has been further and further proved in the explanation of each successive chord, but as regards also its scope of modulation. Thus, when once the primitive simplicity of the diatonic style is variegated by the admission of the chromatic element, all the keys that are relative to a minor key are, in an extended sense, also relative to the major key of the same tonic, whence modulations to them are made with admirable effect.

Besides these, the principle of harmonics unfolds a new chain of affinities and brings a new circle of tonalities within the bond of relationship. The major 3rd is so important a harmonic, that the mediant of a major key is a note as important in the key as it is characteristic of it. This major 3rd is therefore beautifully employed as the centre of a new tonal system, the connexion of which with the principal key is attested by the harmonic prominence of the major 3rd of that original tonic. Thus, when the major 3rd of one chord is the root of another,

[a] Page 116.

and when the major 3rd of one chord is the 5th of another,

each two of these have a most remarkable affinity, and the progression from the first to the second chord in each case has an effect as peculiar as it is natural and beautiful. Extending this relationship from chords to keys, the modulation from any major key to that of which its 3rd is the tonic, or to that of which its 3rd is the dominant, is employed with excellent effect. For examples of this let me refer you to the Allegro Con Brio in Beethoven's Sonata, Op. 53, to his great Overture to Leonore, and to the "Kyrie" in his first Mass, all of which are in C, and all of which have that portion of the movement in E (the 3rd of the original key) which, in most other cases, stands in the key of the dominant; and, again, to the same composer's great Sonata, Op. 106, which is ♭B, and has that portion of the movement in G (of which D, the 3rd of ♭B, is the dominant) that usually stands in the 5th of the original key; and to his Violin Quintet in C, where the key of A is employed in the same relative sense.

The first chromatic concord that was named to you, was the chord of the minor 2nd of the key, the chord of ♭D in the key of C, for instance.* This chord has so intimate a connexion with the tonic, in the minor

---

* Page 109.

key especially, that it sometimes becomes itself a key-note for a transient modulation. Very striking illustrations of the singularly beautiful effect of this transition are to be found in the Allegro Assai in Beethoven's Sonata, Op. 57, which, being in F minor, modulates after the very first phrase into the key of ♭G; to his Quartet in E minor, Op. 59, the first Allegro of which modulates into ♮F at the same period of the movement; and to the Andante in Mendelssohn's Octet, which, being in C minor, modulates also at the same period into ♭D. There is something so remote in the sound, yet so relative in the coherence—so dissimilar in character, yet so united in tonality by the one chord which in all three examples effects the return to the original tonic—that the peculiar expression conveyed by the transition I have been describing stands quite apart from all the rest of a musician's resources.

Truth is single. This Spenser has pointedly symbolized in naming his heroine Una, who is the personification of verity. A notable evidence, then, of the truth of Alfred Day's theory of harmony, is that perfect unity prevails throughout it; and in this respect it differs from every other of the many I have studied. Let me place this unity distinctly before your apprehension by rapidly reviewing the several points of the whole system. *Unity of Day's theory*

The ancient style is distinguished from the modern, and the rules for each are shown to be clear, consistent, and comprehensive. The confusion that prevails in many minds as to what are the limits of the elder, and the extent of the later style, may be dispelled by an observance of this distinction.

The ancient, contrapuntal, strict or diatonic style, regards the interval of the 4th from the bass as invariably dissonant; allows of no unprepared discords, save only passing-notes; and applies its uniform rules of progression and combination equally and alike to all the notes of the key, admitting not the inflection of any of these, save in the special cases stated in our second lecture.

The modern, fundamental, free or chromatic style, admits inflected notes that change not the key; acknowledges exceptional treatment of certain notes in the key as distinct from others, which is exemplified by the second inversion—including the consonant 4th—of three exceptional chords, and by the selection of three exceptional notes as roots of fundamental harmonies; and accepts the natural generation of discords in place of their artificial preparation.

The rules for concords and for the three classes of discords—passing-notes, suspensions, and essential discords—in the strict style, are general, uniform and exceptionless.

The rules for concords and discords in the free style are special to particular notes, having always a reference to the relationship of each to the tonic. The exceptional treatment of the concords of the keynote, the subdominant and the dominant, refers to this relationship; the treatment of each of the chromatic concords refers to and depends upon this relationship; the natural resolutions of each and all of the chromatic discords refer to this relationship.

And now we have to consider the harmonic theory to the unity in which I particularly desire to draw your attention. The root and 5th—the perfect, inflexible notes—in every fundamental chord, are ever free in their treatment. The major 3rd, the most sensitive note in the harmonic series, evinces its keenly sensitive character no less when it is heard in the dominant common chord, or in the chromatic concord of the supertonic, than when it is combined in the most extreme available discords. The 7th is, in the simplest forms of harmony to which it belongs, a discord; its dissonant character is unchanged, and its treatment is unaffected by the addition of any new element to the chord; and it loses its character of a discord, and it is enfranchised from its resolutionary restrictions, only when the root and 3rd are omitted from the chord—the two notes with which it forms a dissonance. The minor or major 9th is resolvable while the rest of the chord remains; it is resolvable also, with the change of the entire harmony, upon a note of another chord, and its dissonance, like that of the 7th, is with the notes below it in the harmonic series, irrespective of those of higher number. The 11th can be resolved on a note of the same chord, after the manner of the 9th; and it too can be resolved on the note of another chord. The minor or major 13th, following the rule of the

11th and the 9th, may be resolved on a note of the same chord; and, again, following the other rule of those same notes, it may be resolved on a note having a different root from its own. Here it should be plain that the freedom of any note, or the law that governs its treatment, is permanent, and wholly unqualified by the introduction of any higher notes of the harmonic series, or by the rules that refer to them. And hence, the laws of every successively added discord are, as one after another we master their knowledge, each an additional store to our theoretical attainments, each confirming and strengthening all that we knew before, and never setting aside, or over-riding, or in any degree qualifying, the rules previously mastered. Even in the compound chords of the augmented 6th, the treatment of the notes belonging either to the primary or to the secondary root is uninfluenced by the presence of those notes which are peculiar to the other of these two roots;[*] that is, the 9th of the dominant follows the same rule that it would were the notes derived from the supertonic not sounded; and the 3rd, 7th, and 9th of the supertonic are treated as if the dominant 9th were absent from the chord. Lastly, the imperfect harmonies that seem at variance with the strict

---

[*] A better analogy than this of two roots for the several series of harmonics from one generator that are employed together in the interval of the augmented 6th with its accompanying notes, would be to describe them as the limbs of a fork into which a trunk often divides, the said one trunk with its root being common to both limbs and all their branches.

uniformity of the diatonic style, but which are obstinately inevitable save by a quasi-compromise of the diatonic principle—such as the flattening of the 7th of the key—are all accounted for by the harmonic theory; since the chord of the 6th—so called by contrapuntists—upon the supertonic is an incomplete chord of the dominant 7th, the chord of the 6th with the minor 3rd upon the subdominant is an incomplete chord of the dominant minor 9th, and the suspension of the augmented or perfect 5th over the mediant of the minor or the major key is the last inversion of the minor or major 13th.

Such is the unity which, as I have said, proves the truth of this harmonic theory. It is onefold throughout; and its simplicity makes it as clear of comprehension as it is easy of application. Further, I have quoted abundant examples to establish beyond question that the theory is in accordance with the practice of the great masters, and these examples might have been multiplied vastly beyond the limits of present time and patience for their attention. It has been indeed ever the province of the artist, the man of imagination, to invent, or—shall I use the other form of the same word?—to discover, the elements of the beautiful; and the province of the theorist, the man of reflection, to explain and systematize and account for these discoveries, and thus render their use patent to all coming time. It still remains for genius to make new applications of the principles this system enunciates; music is a free art, and the period never can arrive when men may say that its resources are exhausted, and that in its exercise the capabilities of the artist's imagination are completed; but I firmly believe that everything which may be hereafter written with good effect, like everything which has up to the present time been produced, will be, must be, clearly accountable and fully explicable by the theory it has been my privilege to lay before you.

<small>Discrepancies in notation.</small>

I know well, nobody better, that objection to this theory may be made on the ground of the names it assigns to certain notes in the key, and consequently to certain notes in the chords in such key. It must here be noticed, however, that there is complete contrariety between the practice of violinists and the principle of mathematicians as to whether the note of higher or lower name, in the enharmonic diesis, be the higher or lower in pitch; men of science proving that, for example, $\flat$E is an acuter sound than $\sharp$D, but string instrument players choosing, on the contrary, to intonate $\sharp$D sharper than $\flat$E. This antagonism between choice and proof, between practice and principle, between art and science, is I believe of comparatively recent growth; but the general ear has become so habituated to the effect it constantly experiences, has become so trained to expect what it constantly receives, that string instrument players, and singers too, must needs now feed the appetite they have created. Let me mention a curious case in which truth had to give place to custom in this very particular; before equal temperament was adopted in the tuning of the Temple organ, the black keys of that instrument were divided so as to open different pipes for the two notes which are represented on the pianoforte by one key; and Mr. Hopkins, the organist, has assured me that, in order to assimilate his accompaniment to the intonation of the choir, it was necessary for him to play the contrary note to that which was on paper, sounding ♯D where ♭E was written, and making ♭E speak when ♯D was the note of the chord.

This objection manifestly applies to the notation of the supertonic minor 9th and the dominant minor 13th, which notes, as I have freely shown, are as commonly written by the great masters, even in repetitions of the same passages, by the lower as by the higher of their alphabetical names. It would be as logical to urge the same objection to the harmonic appropriation of the intervals of the minor 7th and the 11th; because, although there can be no question of the names of these notes, the universal practice of all singers and players, of all instrument makers, and of all tuners, is to intonate these notes differently from their true harmonic sound. The minor 7th of nature is somewhat flatter, and the 11th somewhat sharper than the notes rendered in musical performance, which from custom the ear accepts as correct; and players on brass instruments—which, as I long since stated, naturally sound no notes but their harmonics —are obliged to have recourse to some artifice for sharpening the 7th and flattening the 11th, in order to render these notes available for combination with the rest of the orchestra. That it is an abnormal condition of the musical sense to tolerate, nay, to look for these qualified 7ths and 11ths—that this condition shows us to be in a state of cultivation and not a state of Nature—is proved by an interesting passage in Spohr's Autobiography, wherein he gives an account of his observations, and the observations of such a musician compel our respect, of the music of the Swiss peasantry. Every one of you has heard of their custom of calling together their cattle by playing on the horn; every one is familiar with the term Ranz des Vaches that defines the melodies they play, whose peculiarity results from their being composed of the harmonic notes of the horn on which they are played. These notes are sounded without sophistication in Switzerland, the horn players there having no regard for the civilized intonation of the orchestra, or the drawing-room. Such of the peasantry as do not play, regard the notes of the horn as their musical standard, since probably they hear no other instrument; and, their ear being thus tutored, they habitually sing their minor 7th so flat and their 11th so sharp (the horn players have not the skill to produce the higher harmonics) that they would be inadmissible into cultivated musical society.

Although, as I believe, the practice be modern of reversing the intonation of the enharmonic diesis—more recent certainly than the building of the Temple organ by Renato Harris—the discrepancy between the desire of the tutored ear and the prescription of science has prevailed since the time of the Greek theorists, who waged violent disputes on this very subject. Pythagoras, the first philosopher, made elaborate calculations by which he divided the degrees of the scale. Two centuries later, Aristoxenus, who has been called the father of temperament, professed that oral impression and not arithmetical calculation should be the test of the truthful intonation of these gradual divisions. Two strongly opposed parties supported these various theories; the Pythagoreans contending that calculation was infallible, and that the ear should be schooled to the perception and the acceptance of truth; the Aristoxenians protesting that the natural sense was the best interpreter of the principles of nature, and that the results of calculation should be modified so as to meet the requirements of the ear.

Let us turn from music to other arts, and we shall find a like disparity between what Nature gives and that which is changed by cultivation. Do we not increase the complexity and diversify the colours of our flowers? Do we not augment the nourishment and enrich the taste of our fruits? Do we not extract bread and beer and the strongest forms of alcohol from what, but for cultivation, are the meanest of grasses? Do we not adorn—in spite of Thomson's often quoted line—our own natures? But all these, you may retort, are not fine arts, and afford no analogy to music. Turn then to poetry and painting, music's acknowledged sisters. What is verse but a refinement upon natural speech? Who would be content with a picture that represented its objects with the faithfulness of a looking-glass, without the temperament they receive from the painter's imagination? And where is, or ever has been, the human form so divinely perfect as it is shown in the masterpieces of sculpture?

After all, enough has been said of the occasional expediency of false notation, and enough has been shown of the sensuous faculty of adjusting tempered sounds so that we hear them as what they should be rather than as what they are, to prove that this question of notation is of small import to practice or to effect. It is of deep, of infinite import, however, to theory; since the name of a note refers it to its derivation, and thus entirely controls its treatment. It is of the utmost consequence, then, that a composer should know and thoroughly feel the radical derivation of every note he writes, which I believe to be distinctly traceable by the theory I have explained; and knowing this, it is for him to exercise what discretion he may in meeting the convenience of those who read his music, by writing his chords and his passing-notes so that they may look the most familiar and cost the fewest accidentals.

Conclusion. In conclusion let me state that, while I have attempted to give you a general insight into the principles of harmony, I by no means pretend to have made in this Course of Lectures a complete exposition of all the laws that constitute what might be called the syntax of music. To have done so would have greatly exceeded the limits of any six meetings, and the comprehension of any audience who had not the opportunity of making their own practical exemplification of every rule that was enunciated. The object has been to assist, if might be, the musical tendency now obvious in this country, by spreading a knowledge of the materials out of which the greatest artists have wrought their masterpieces. I believe that such knowledge is an essential aid to the perception of the beautiful; although I am well aware that, when an ultimate technical analysis of any work of art has been made, the profoundest critic is utterly unable to define in what its true beauty consists, in what it has the power to pass from the senses to the heart, and make us more than know, make us feel its preternatural qualities. Beauty is as insusceptible of definition as is the phenomenon of chemical action or the miracle of life. The perception of this wonderful, mysterious, subtle essence in any artistic production must still rest with our own most delicate faculties when all the ingredients of the work have been most minutely sifted, when every principle that directs their construction has been explained; but I speak from experience when I say that these faculties may be refined by study, and I shall suppose that your time with me may not have been misspent, if what has been said here may stimulate you to make further inquiry into the subject than the circumstances of these lectures could enable me to satisfy. It is no more to be wished that every person who learns harmony should become a composer, than that every person who learns English should become a poet—Providence protect us from the reams of rubbish that would ensue upon either contingency! But as we learn to discriminate the elements of language in order to the understanding of the best books that have been written, so we learn to analyse the essentials of music in order to the comprehension of the greatest works in the art.

THE END.

PRINTED BY BALLANTYNE, HANSON AND CO.
LONDON AND EDINBURGH

www.ingramcontent.com/pod-product-compliance
Lightning Source LLC
Chambersburg PA
CBHW021806230426
43669CB00008B/649